ASPERGERS AND THE INFANT CHILD

How to recognise the signs; starting school and problems encountered; practical advice for parents/teachers.

COLETTE McCoy
Special Needs Teacher and Mother

authorHOUSE®

AuthorHouse™ UK Ltd.
500 Avebury Boulevard
Central Milton Keynes, MK9 2BE
www.authorhouse.co.uk
Phone: 08001974150

First published by AuthorHouse 8/30/2011

ISBN: 978-1-4567-8975-6 (sc)
ISBN: 978-1-4567-8976-3 (e)

To our lovely Elizabeth, for whom it all has been worth while; may you continue to be 'quirky' forevermore, we love you just the way you are!

Acknowledgements

To so many people who have helped my daughter and our family: the doctors, nurses, health visitors, paediatrician and speech therapists.

Special thanks to all those at Premier Nursery, the Pre-School S.E.N.Co (Special Educational Needs Co-ordinator), members of my local authority advisory inclusion service, the A.S.D. link nurse, Parent Partnership and the fantastic O.S.S.M.E. (Outreach Support Service for Mainstream Education)/Autism Initiatives team. Heartfelt thanks to the various teachers, teaching and welfare assistants, S.E.N.Co and Head teacher at Elizabeth's school.

Sincere thanks to all my friends and family who have had to listen to my concerns/rants; particularly my various S.E.N. (Special Educational Needs) colleagues, who have been a position to provide me with the best advice.

Finally, to my husband for pointing out "What if she is?" when her condition came to light and my son (a.k.a. Cuddles) for just being a kind and thoughtful boy who looks after his sister.

Foreword

I have been a teacher for many years now- I began as an English and Drama teacher, before promotion to Head of Drama and Second in English. I was always keen to teach children of all abilities and really liked making a difference to those who needed extra support. I trained to teach children with specific learning difficulties and after I had my son (and later my daughter) I returned to teaching three days a week, as a Specific Learning Difficulties Teacher.

So, I was a S.E.N. teacher before I had my daughter. That did not mean I was prepared for all aspergers entails, or indeed looked for it- the exact opposite, if I am honest. I did not want to label my daughter at all, certainly not at such an early age. The health visitors, speech therapists, nursery workers and L.E.A. (Local Education Authority) support workers constantly hinted at what I really already knew, deep down.

I particularly remember an excellent nursery worker trying to hint to me; rather afraid of saying what she meant clearly, in case I was offended. Then, one day she described a child who was obviously on the autistic spectrum and I would professionally have said that they were. That child was my Elizabeth. In the end I said, "It is okay, you can just say it- she has autistic tendencies/she is aspergers."

I then undertook an A.S.D. (Autistic Syndrome Disorder) course that traced autism from birth and as I saw example after example, I 'saw' my child in every one. There was 'nowhere to hide' after that. However, I still remember her 'diagnosis,' it was as if she had some sort of disease- "Your daughter has aspergers." There isn't anything 'wrong' with her, she isn't ill; she is aspergers, she hasn't 'got it' -like a fatal disease. I felt lucky that she wasn't ill, some people have far more to contend with, I thought. So, why did I cry?

This book details Elizabeth's journey (and that of our family) but also provides valuable information for all families of children touched by aspergers. It is also written as a mother and teacher because I wanted to give both points of view. I have found many asperger books to be of a clinical nature and parents are often just given a diagnosis; without subsequent advice and support. In my experience, it is like throwing a grenade and then running away- whilst families are left to deal with the fall-out!

Hopefully, this book is accessible for all and may help people- it has certainly helped me and when Elizabeth is older, I hope it will explain a few things to her. I also hope that it will enlighten professionals who work with her (and others like her.) My point is that I am the closest person to my daughter and I don't fully know or understand her. Some people have told me that they know how she is feeling. How can anyone know how she is feeling? My one hope for her is that she learns to understand and accept herself for who she is and that we give her all the love, patience and confidence which will put her on the correct path in life. Fingers crossed!

Table of Contents

PART ONE -

Specific Traits of Aspergers - Elizabeth's story

It's going to be a long night…the sort of night that any mother with a sick child knows about, all too well. A night of little sleep, tears, as an infection takes hold. Only Mummy will do as Daddy's attempts to pacify have failed- within ten minutes she is smiling and wants us to be 'girls with heads together' on the pillow. We talk and hold hands for hours, until sleep… I lie and look at my beautiful daughter, Elizabeth, and think that these hard times are strangely some of the best memories a mother has- of being so close to your child, who you then watch sleeping. For me, with Elizabeth, there were few times like these.

I Hear The Beginning Is A Good Place To Start…

My daughter was 'different' from birth. She was born after a difficult pregnancy; where she was lying laterally, the wrong way for birth, from my first twelve week scan. My son's birth two years previously, and the pregnancy, had also been challenging as I had a condition where I aborted the foetus and had had previous miscarriages. My son, Alex, was okay but after days of labour and an emergency caesarean I had a large baby who was two weeks late; he created much space for his sister to occupy two years later.

Hence, at thirty six weeks pregnant with Elizabeth a doctor ordered me to pack my things and go to hospital as they could n't risk my life and that of my unborn baby. I sobbed, worried for my unborn child and not wanting to be parted from my son and husband.

Finally, Elizabeth was born over two weeks early by caesarean- it took many surgeons to remove her as she was embedded and I thought I'd lost her. I went down to surgery (for prep) at 9:00 am and she finally emerged kicking and screaming, at 11:02 am when the Head Consultant finally succeeded in his mission. I spent the whole afternoon vomiting and shaking whilst Elizabeth slept for twelve hours.

My daughter seemed to smile all the time from the next day onwards. She was perfect; still weighing 7lb 5ozs, even though she was early. She fed well, breastfeeding for a while and eventually sleeping through the night.

The First Signs

When a baby is four months old things seem to get easier, it did with my son. A routine is developed. However, I was beginning to notice Elizabeth was resisting day time sleeping. She would nap for ten minutes at a time. I would lie down with her and stroke her face (always worked for my son!) but she just looked at me as if to say, "What do you think you are doing? That won't work with me!" She would become very irritable during the day and was n't a cuddly child at all. I must admit that I found this tremendously difficult, the closeness was n't really the same as with my son.

My husband would come home from work and I'd be exhausted and he'd say jokingly, "Oh, she is n't like that, she's a good girl." You know when you want to strangle someone?

I decided to join the gym and get fit so that I would have more energy for my daughter. So, five month old Elizabeth would attend the crèche at the gym for an hour and as I had to pay for it, and the class, I got into a routine; even though at times I must have looked like a walking corpse.

By the time Elizabeth was eight months old I was totally exhausted, she still only napped for ten minutes at a time and did not always sleep right through at night time (I was still on extended maternity leave.) She was irritable and continued to push me away. The Health Visitor called and told me to just persevere and leave her in the cot. So, I would put her in the cot, close the door and persist. The door could never be left open. She eventually slept and I had an afternoon nap but in my own bed; she just would not sleep in the same bed as me. However, if she was in our bed (on the very few occasions that she was ill) she would chat for hours and hours…Elizabeth could stay awake longer than anyone of us in the house, we called her the 'Duracell bunny!'

Early Concerns

Elizabeth attended nursery for three days when I returned to teaching; she was now ten and a half months old. It became apparent that she always preferred solitary play, her toys would be lined up and she would become upset if things were moved. Also, she seemed to like her routine, her house and belongings. Elizabeth would sit with jigsaws and I would sit down in her little space- I had to penetrate her world as she distanced herself; only if she really wanted something would she bother with me! So, I merely passed the jigsaw pieces to her.

On the few occasions when her father would go away overnight on business it really was 'out of sight, out of mind.' She did not want to know him when he arrived back, eager to see her. It was around this time that my darling daughter decided that she did not want to go to sleep in the afternoon. I persisted… until one afternoon she soiled her nappy, took it off and swung it around the bedroom. I know you can imagine the mess. However, she was sat there rather defiantly waiting for me to discover the horror!

Obsessive Behaviour and can it be changed?

Then there was Elizabeth's obsessive behaviour. Clothes were a problem, anything happening to them - creasing or spoiling. She loved to play out, was always very physical, and I was happy for her to come home with signs that she had had a good day! However, she loved 'girly' dresses and extra clothes for emergencies would often be used. Elizabeth would say that there was a mark on her clothes and become so single-minded and obsessed that she would continually beg (annoy) the girls at the nursery to change her. They would repeatedly explain that there was n't a mark but she would be so pre-occupied and upset that they would change her.. and change her...

So, I sat my daughter down and told her that the girls could not spend all day changing her. I said that she could not wear dresses anymore for nursery. Hence, I forced her to wear trousers. She kicked and screamed but I persisted. She did not like this arrangement, one little bit but three weeks later we agreed that she could wear a dress for nursery which was not allowed to be changed. It all went well. This was probably why the nursery then reported that messy play was her least favourite activity- the sand and water could spill onto her and the clothes!

There will always be the problem at this age- what is aspergers and what is just a child's character? I have seen many parents just give in to tantrums and some persist despite the child's constant agitation. We all make mistakes and there have been times when I have shouted at Elizabeth when I should n't have. However, it was important to me that she had a sense of discipline.

What I am trying to say is that I believe that some A.S.D. tendencies can be managed, or even changed, at an early age; if they are identified and challenged in the correct manner. A.S.D. is a continuum from mild to acute - most of us struggle from one episode to another in the life of a child with A.S.D. as each child can be so different.

Sharing/Turn-Taking, or Not! Strategies I tried.

Another such 'episode' in Elizabeth's life was sharing...or not. She did not socialise well with other children and would play by herself, even at home, so sharing was a non-existent skill. I would sit by my daughter, pass her the various jigsaw pieces and interact with her but she was very solitary. Trying to interact with her when she did n't want me to or introducing anything that was new, was difficult. When I wanted her to eat fruit, I would cut up the pineapple, put it in a small bowl and eat it myself and then she would show some interest. She might approach me but if I offered her some she would not respond. So, I would leave the bowl on a little toy box and possibly leave the room. It was rather like animals feeding in the wild!

The sharing issue eventually came to a head at nursery when Elizabeth only wanted to watch a DVD that she chose, despite what others wanted. Negotiation is not a concept that children with aspergers understand as they only see the world through their own eyes. However, wanting to prepare my daughter for living in the real world I told the nursery to adopt our house rule- the DVD could not be watched unless all children agreed; any arguments and the television would be switched off. This worked well.

When sharing was forced upon Elizabeth, this acted as a trigger of upset. On one occasion she was building a tower with foam blocks and was taking all the blue ones. Another child sat next to her and placed a different colour on the tower. Elizabeth shouted, "No!" and took it off. The other child put another block on the tower again and Elizabeth knocked the tower over and grabbed all of the blue bricks to keep for herself. A target was set for her: to include another child in building a structure and to take it in turns to place a brick. The nursery worked on this target with her and we were so lucky that there was such caring and knowledgeable staff to aid our daughter.

It was also noted that Elizabeth began to 'perform,' she would sing a solo song when asked but would not be interested when another child had a turn- she would just walk off. This illustrates how self-centred aspergers children can be.

Solitary Play

Parties were a time when Elizabeth's tendency for solitary play became particularly evident. When it was time to sit down she was always the last to do so as she had been so absorbed in her play and was unsure how to behave at the party table. I remember at one party she sat herself between two girls who were best friends and holding hands; they were unhappy but she did not understand or even notice the girls' reactions.

Elizabeth became very attached to her belongings, especially her toy 'Mousey.' When she was upset she would say that she needed the toy. She would sit with all of her toys around her, in her bed, and would be agitated if something was missing. Often, the same toys would be lined up and could not be moved, if they were she would have to re-arrange them to be in their original places.

Barbie dolls were a favourite plaything. Elizabeth did begin to talk to the Barbie dolls and to communicate through toys; something that she still does today! If I need to know how she is really feeling the toys may be able to tell me!

Particular books would be taken to bed, such as 'We're Going On A Bear Hunt.' She loved her pink bookcase, collecting books and would hold them tightly in bed. DVDs would also be played repetitively. She loved many, including 'The Wizard Of Oz' and she would repeat the lines and eventually role play some of the scenes. When she was collected from nursery she usually wanted to go straight home- she always loved the familiarity of home and would escape into The Land Of Oz.

The nursery would provide enlightening observations concerning Elizabeth. One time she was observed playing with the dolls and placing them, one at a time, into a car. She then pushed the car up and down before taking all the dolls out. Then, she repeated the process all afternoon. Other children were playing together and occasionally she would glance at them but then continue with what she was doing. Most children would want to play with others and be intrigued by what they were doing but she could not be distracted. She would need to be prompted by an adult to help her move from one solitary activity to another.

Children do get upset but calm down, often due to a distraction which takes their mind away from the situation that caused upset. Aspergers children are obsessive, focused and do not calm down easily. So if you then shout because they should be able to stop, the situation is made worse and they can be terrified by the noise and cry forever...

Problems Understanding People and Situations

Role play was something she loved, via dressing up. It was about this time that it became quite clear that she had problems understanding characters. Little Miss Naughty was the good girl and Little Miss Sunshine could be quite naughty; some little tiny detail in the story would ensure that she acquired the wrong idea in her head.

Once, whilst watching Lilo and Stitch, a group of girls, led by a ginger-haired girl (Mildred) were being horrid to Lilo because she was 'different.' Elizabeth watched the DVD constantly for weeks and was unable to see that the girls were being unkind. In the film, Lilo and Stitch steal the girl's bike and Elizabeth, rightly, saw that that was wrong. However, she still could not see that Lilo behaved so because of the girls' cruelty.

Not understanding when children were being cruel happened frequently with my daughter. She did not understand when a friend was playing with her cousin that she did not want to play with her. She followed the two around and it was quite sad to witness how children can be so cruel; for once I was glad that she did not understand.

The truth was that Elizabeth was not a very good friend, herself. Having friends as guests to play was very problematic as she would just sit and play away from a friend who came to visit; only bothering with them when she felt like it. The friend would talk to me instead; I had to keep them entertained and stop arguments when she refused to share. I felt I should side with the other child as I did not want my daughter to always get her own way. It was only when she was four that she had a quiet best friend. However, she had to then play exclusively with this child and not others at the same time. If this friend was absent Elizabeth would always revert back to solitary play.

When we went for family meals, she would bring a toy which she liked to sit with its legs crossed. On one particular occasion it was placed off the table and I thought that I would see how long she would obsess over the legs not being crossed. Forty-five minutes later she asked me to reach the doll and put its legs 'right.' She would then talk 'through' her toys in the third person and talk about things like they happened yesterday, when they could have occurred a few months ago. The concept of time seemed to confuse her.

Living with a child who is aspergers you learn quickly to pre-empt situations. Like many parents, I often learnt the hard way. One Saturday, shopping in Southport, was a classic example. A visit to Claire's accessories (a classic 'girly' shop) was such an occasion. The lady gave my daughter a net basket, whilst I was looking at the jewellery. It was, of course, to put purchases in, not to keep. If I had known what was about to follow I would have clearly explained this; what a wonderful thing hindsight is! Elizabeth seemed very upset when we exited the shop and, at this stage, her language skills were poor so she could not articulate her feelings to me easily. I assumed that she had liked the shop so much that she had not wanted to leave. However, after thirty minutes of non-stop tears, I was still trying to ascertain why she was sobbing. When you want a nice, quiet enjoyable day it just gets spoilt! Fifteen minutes later, she calmed down enough to say the words, "Lady took my bag." In her eyes she had been given the bag by one kind lady and another person took it away from her. Note to self: be more vigilant; if you see a lady bearing a bag you must point out that it is not the child's bag, just there to put purchases in! So long as you tell Elizabeth before something happens she can usually cope.

Hobbies were always a case in point. If I took Elizabeth swimming I had to be quite clear where we were going and for how long. Small group swimming lessons began very badly as she could not focus and would always drift away and have to be brought back. The teacher did not have to tell me that my daughter was not getting much out of these lessons; she nicely suggested I take her elsewhere as she was taking up too much of her time, quite rightly, as she had other children in the group.

We decided upon paying a private instructor to teach both of our children, together; costly, but necessary. This did not work as Elizabeth just required too much attention and just wanted to play. So, after one lesson, Alex continued with the 1:1 lessons whilst I swam with Elizabeth for half an hour; I kept her away from her brother but after the lesson we would all have some time in the pool for playing together.

It was only when the private instructor stopped undertaking 1:1 lessons that Elizabeth tried small group lessons again, a year later. They did not begin so well as she would not join in, preferring to play nearby, instead. I informed the instructors that she had aspergers, (although she had not been formally diagnosed) but after being in the pool with her for ten minutes they could see for themselves that all was not quite as it should be. After a while she joined in and I would reinforce that she had to do 'good listening' with the instructor. Later, she had a new instructor who was always there every week and she was fantastic with Elizabeth- the routine and environment meant that she eventually settled in.

Ballet was another hobby that required special attention. The teacher never really knew if my daughter did not understand or was taking advantage. However, I told her to air on the side of caution with regards to discipline. Then when she was nearly ready to move up a class she could not skip. Well, she would not believe that it was skipping as she had something else in her mind that she thought it was. So, I skipped everywhere with her until she believed me.

Real Language Difficulties and Speech and Language Therapy

Elizabeth did not say much, unless she wanted something; then she would use single words- for example, "Food!" Health visitors usually make a routine call at eighteen months old, but Elizabeth was nearly two when the professional came. Now, my daughter was not a 'performing seal' and did not take to strangers well so it did not go according to plan. She just sat there and did not complete anything she was asked to do!

It was plain that she did not know many words- pointing at pictures she would say 'car' for 'van' or 'ambulance.' What was apparent was the fact that once she believed something was a certain thing, her mind could not be changed. Hence, she had to 're-learn' many of the words that she actually thought that she knew.

She was to be re-evaluated by the Health Visitor at three monthly intervals. I thought that she was a little young for speech therapy as, in my experience, vocabulary needs time to blossom. Eventually, she went on a waiting list and was seen when she was three years old; an initial consultation which showed poor vocabulary skills. She was asked to attend within another six months but unfortunately, due to a lack of speech therapists, she was not seen. Officials from Children's Services eventually pressed for her to be seen in the January, when she would be four in the April. She attended speech therapy sessions, every week for eight weeks and I followed a program at home. This all involved good sitting, listening and looking (difficult as she could not sustain eye contact) picture cards and posting visual pictures when activities were completed (see part three later for guidance.)

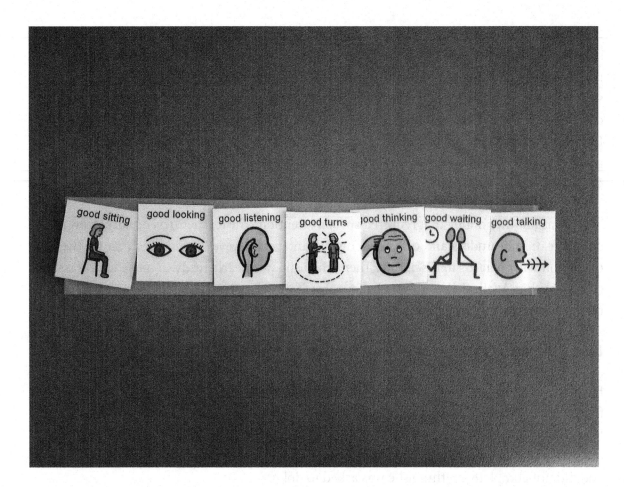

This went well and we really focused upon taking turns, at home. This did not go so well when my husband tried board games with her. It appeared that games with four players was just too much waiting for her to sustain her interest. The speech therapist did remark that Elizabeth could remain on task, if she was interested, and referred her to the paediatrician for A.D.H.D. (Attention Disorder Hyperactivity Syndrome- yet another label) and we then had to wait for an appointment.

By now a pre-school S.E.N.Co was involved who was advising nursery on strategies to help Elizabeth and the nursery undertook the speech therapy program with her; in consultation with the speech therapist and myself as I was following the same program at home with my daughter. She would not say many words that people could understand and repeated what people said all of the time; this is known as 'Echolalia.' Nursery observed on 17th September 2007 that she was playing in the sand tray and filling a bucket with another child; the latter said, "It's bigger" and Elizabeth merely parroted these words.

It was about this time that a hearing test was suggested to ensure that she could hear instruction- it proved that she could. Staff in the nursery were uncertain about Elizabeth's understanding of questions as other children would tend to respond for her and then she would merely imitate their words. This did not happen at home- she would not let her brother speak for her and we never encouraged him to do so. This lack of independence occurred in toileting because, both at home and nursery, she would go to the toilet but stay there until an adult reminded her to come out. So, she was given a toilet buddy in nursery and would leave the toilet when the other child would prompt her to leave.

A target from nursery, around this time, was for her to speak first in a conversation. However, she did not (and was reluctant to) know how to initiate a conversation- she would have to be taught that which comes naturally to so many.

At home I would work on non-verbal communication with Elizabeth such as facial expression, eye contact and physical space. So smiling at people and standing near to them (but not on top of them!) was essential. Then, what to say- such as, "Hello" and telling a child her name and then asking what their name was. She would prefer to stay with the one friend who knew her; with time it would improve, I had faith in that- when she was ready to be more independent we would focus on this area again.

There were great concerns over Elizabeth's speech and language development. Adults who knew her well could interpret some of her speech but generally it was difficult to understand. Her understanding of language was poor, she therefore avoided social interaction and a vicious circle developed.

Elizabeth did begin to start asking "Why?" questions, but would not listen to the answers; I don't think she actually internalised them for a long time and I am not sure to what extent she still does. I worked on speech and language work with her and she learnt to respond to one step instructions- such as, "Put your shoes on." At times Elizabeth did not connect events- "We are going outside so you have to put your shoes on!" All steps would have to be broken down for her, not given to her together- such as, "We are going to the park, put your shoes and coat on." Too much information, which would result in confusion!

Elizabeth and I attended a speech and language therapy block every Friday throughout January and February 2008 and this was continued at home and within nursery every day. Visual cards were used to reinforce social rules- so a picture of an ear meant good listening and a person sat on a chair at a table was good sitting, for example. The support program was aimed at developing turn-taking, to build attention and listening skills and understanding/ answering open-ended questions. I would model appropriate responses for her and an aim was for her to follow an adult's lead and stay focused- to learn from and use the structured praise of good sitting and good looking, via a visual timetable (see part 3.) At home we focused upon taking turns and I invited children to our home to encourage Elizabeth's social interaction.

At this point the Speech and Language Therapist made a referral to the Community Paediatrician to gain further opinion concerning Elizabeth's poor attention and high activity levels. Speech and Language Therapy would be involved in her transition to primary school as she would require some support with following daily routines and listening to instructions.

In July 2008 Elizabeth's communication skills were examined again. Listening and attention skills were poor as she was easily distracted and needed visual and verbal prompts to re-focus her attention. As a result, this meant that she often missed vital parts of information in instructions. In the classroom Elizabeth was going to need extra teacher explanation and visual aids to pre-empt problems.

Elizabeth's receptive language (what she understands) showed that she had difficulty demonstrating that she had understood the requests. She could point at pictures but would not include any details that were asked of her and so no age equivalent score could be reached. Another less formal test did show an age equivalent score of 2 years 6 months and she was now 4 years 2 months old. Elizabeth's expressive language (what she says) was assessed by being able to name single items presented in pictures; this had greatly improved and was at a 3 year and 8 month level.

Elizabeth's last speech therapy assessment was in February 2010 and her receptive language showed linguistic concepts as above average; basic concepts and sentence structure at average for her age. She was shown a series of pictures and had to follow the given instruction in relation to them. Her expressive language showed a 5 year 10-11 month level and so was age appropriate. An additional test showed that her language associated with grammar was at the level 5 year-5 months and information at 7 year-5 months- Elizabeth was now 5 year 10 months old.

Such fantastic improvements mean that a child is only reviewed annually until the service is no longer needed. Elizabeth could identify some emotions from picture cards but did not understand more subtle ones. I was sent another booklet to follow with her (see part 3)- the same emotions booklet that I had covered twice with her already!

The Realisation of A.S.D.

The nursery's key worker was becoming increasingly concerned about Elizabeth's social interaction and I would continually be told about the next problem/strange occurrence upon my return from work. I knew because I was a special needs teacher that the key worker was hinting at aspergers, but I think because of that she was reticent to say the actual words. I said that Elizabeth did display such behaviours but as she was so young only time would tell. I did not want to see problems where there were n't any just because of a label and because I was more aware of aspergers than the average parent. Also, teaching children with special needs was quite different than accepting that your beautiful daughter had such needs- a label just made it all sound so final.

The realisation did set in, in the days after my conversation with Elizabeth's key worker. I had a good cry; it was only Terry, my husband, who said, "What if she has?" Then followed by, "What can I do to help her?" That was probably the best single thing that anyone had said to me concerning Elizabeth's condition. What if she was aspergers? I worked with special needs children and knew the struggles but that did not mean that she could not have a rich, fruitful life. I think that health and happiness come first and the rest is just a bonus. If she was not aspergers then she would not be my Elizabeth; so I would not want to change that, anyway.

Elizabeth first saw the paediatrician about a month after her fourth birthday. There were tests that had to be undertaken- a test for fragile x to see if she had a genetic learning difficulty. He said that she had Pervasive Developmental Delay, Communication and Learning. He also found a heart murmur.

The next day I had to take Elizabeth for blood tests and a heart scan. She was always so well, never ill; I sat and cried when I thought about how I was going to explain to her what would happen when the lady took blood. She kept asking me what was the name of the lady who would be taking the blood; luckily it was the nurse from the previous day at the paediatrician's office. Surprisingly, Elizabeth did not cry as blood was taken, she just seemed to be looking around and examining the situation. The heart scan showed that she had leaky valves, but the results were not made known for months. However, the limit was .045 and she was .038, so she came just within normal limits, to our relief! I must say that I felt that I could take onboard any difficulty so long as she was not medically ill. I felt lucky, just as I always was, to have her as she was.

The paediatrician said that he wanted to see her again by August. Between that May and December her speech progressed and it was the social interaction and processing of information where problems persisted. She was finally seen again in December by the paediatrician and diagnosed with aspergers (Autistic Spectrum Disorder.)

In the classroom Elizabeth was going to need support with pre-empting problems by being given extra information; the preparation/implementation of visual aids and the encouragement to apply skills learnt to other situations throughout the day, would be important to her. A program was provided for school and us, the parents, for September 2008.

In the end, our Local Education Authority asked my family for Elizabeth's details so that she could be added to a Disability Register; which lists children in the area who have a 'disability.' My husband and I were sent the information- if you take that a disability is something which prevents a person from 'normally' carrying out day-to-day activities, then that is fine. Your child needs extra help. However, my husband was horrified by the whole term 'disability' and really thought that it was unnecessary. This was a final acceptance of aspergers and was not easy; what had to follow was arming ourselves with as much knowledge about this condition so we could help our daughter.

Some facts about A.S.D.

So what is Autistic Spectrum Disorder?

Autism affects people in many different ways, from mild to acute - Aspergers is used to describe those at the milder to middle of the spectrum. The National Autistic Society say that there are 535,000 people in this country from all backgrounds and nationalities who have the condition.

Aspergers is not a learning difficulty; people learn differently but many such children are visual learners and this can cause difficulty (see part 3 for information about learning styles and multi-sensory teaching.) Elizabeth will look at something, examine it and learn through this channel- not seeing connections, but in isolation. Hence, she will look at words and merely try to remember them - the word ball; she will not automatically see a connection with call so I have to emphasise it, over and over again until she registers it. Some aspergers children may have an accompanying learning difficulty but, in my experience, I find that most are of average/high ability and not all necessarily mathematical geniuses as often depicted- for example in the film 'Rain Man.'

It is a life-long disability. It is a 'hidden disability;' as it is not a physical disability it does not register automatic understanding. This simply means that people do not see that it exists. It is not a disease or a mental illness. First appearances may present a naughty child whose parents are not instilling discipline- it is not bad parenting.

Aspergers is more common in males and may be because males do not generally talk/listen to each other like females do. It could be linked to: genetics, difficulties at birth or health disorders. By now you are probably thinking that no-one really knows and you would be correct! I don't think it helps my daughter, anyway, or 'makes my day' to hear yet another theory!

It is a series of developmental disorders known as 'The Triad of Impairment,' including:

1. Communication- there may be problems with speech and body language such as gestures, facial expressions and tone of voice. As my daughter cannot 'read' my face jokes/sarcasm are taken literally and she will become agitated and question why I said/did a particular thing. She cannot tell from facial expressions what is happy, sad or angry; the latter really frightens her. We have worked on these and she has improved but can only now grasp some basic facial expressions. Elizabeth also can't always identify her own feelings; so those of others remain a mystery to her!

2. Social interaction- poor social skills/problems with relationships. Elizabeth will take everything literally, "Pull your socks up," means exactly that and I have been informed that she is, in fact, wearing tights. There is a lack of empathy and understanding of others which can result in confusion because of the way other people act. Elizabeth will appear withdrawn/unfriendly without any eye contact but if she does decide to interact she can appear too friendly and stand too close to others. It must be difficult to never get it right but at this age she does n't (thankfully) always sense that others are displeased. I do now explain to her why someone may be thinking something but she won't understand why they do. Yet, understanding that someone is upset is a start.

3. Inflexible thought/imagination- resistance to change and obsessional behaviour. There may be a narrow focus of hobbies- in Elizabeth's case this was collecting jigsaw pieces, yellow fish (long story) and lining up all objects; utter despair/upset if they are then sequenced out of order is my daughter's world. Repetition is key to her world. Elizabeth cannot think about what could happen as she has never experienced it. New experiences can be worrying, for example, due to severe weather her school closed and the change to her routine was difficult for her to take.

All three areas results in aspergers. During the pre-school years delayed development usually occurs when a child is noticeably different than others; I think as a parent you just know!

Important Points Concerning Children With Aspergers and Their Social Communication and Emotional Difficulties- Which May Relate To Your Own Child.

1. Verbal and non-verbal communication- words mean little to some aspergers children so they often do not use them. A child may not respond when you are speaking. Elizabeth can repeat words without any understanding, 'Echolalia' (echo words.)

2. Elizabeth can be unaware of the personal space of others- she can get quite close to the faces of other pupils when talking to them, leaning on them, speaking at normal volume directly into their ear. At school, she taps the teacher's arm to obtain her attention. When she was younger Elizabeth would grab my chin and turn my face to her if she wanted me to listen.

3. Does not recognise/have an interest in peer pressure (for example- do not want the same clothes as other children.) Lacks interest in participating in group activities. I like to think that Elizabeth sets trends and does not follow them!

4. Vulnerable expression of emotion- Elizabeth can show too much distress or affection out of proportion to situations. An aspergers child may need constant reassurance as they can become anxious, especially if events are changed or go wrong.

5. Takes things literally and becomes confused by comments such as, "Pull your socks up." Also, "Stay with your partner" in the computer lesson- when he left his seat to go and ask the teacher something my daughter followed him. Humour/sarcasm can be a minefield for aspergers children as they don't understand them and nothing ruins a joke more than dissecting it and then its purpose still is n't understood! When communicating with others A.S.D. children are vulnerable to bullying due to not understanding situations/people.

6. Elizabeth has difficulty in processing more than one instruction at a time and may interpret them literally. At school, when asked to do two things she completed the first and then just stood there for a few moments; if unsure she follows others. She may not know/understand what work is expected of her. Minimising language during verbal instructions focuses her attention.

7. Handling a two-way conversation. Often an aspergers child does not comment/even appear interested in what another is saying; changes the subject, takes a long time to reply. At school Elizabeth does not always ask for help which can result in her leaving work blank. She can remain passive with boys when in paired work. Some aspergers children speak 'at a tangent' when they are confused/do not understand; we may ask for more information but they merely switch topic.

8. Elizabeth can miss out on some verbal instructions if her name is not used. The teacher has to address her directly- "Raise hands and face the front;" she did not until told, "Elizabeth, face the front." She may miss group verbal instructions if distracted by other pupils or by the lesson content- looking at the computer and the teacher is difficult so she misses instructions. During less structured lesson times she has a shorter attention span, for example at assembly. During time spent practising Christmas songs she did not join in but played with her headband, her fingers or leant across the pupil next to her several times.

9. There are unwritten rules of behaviour- for example, 'snitching' in school is bad. An aspergers child may be unaware of social convention/codes of conduct- inappropriate comments/action and often make personal/hurtful comments without meaning to offend. Elizabeth doesn't know when it is in/appropriate to smile- nobody teaches you such conventions!

10. Expects other people to know what they have experienced when they were not there. Elizabeth will not tell a teaching assistant about her weekend because she knows what she did and assume that others do, too.

11. Cognitive difficulties- inflexible imagination, cannot 'see' future events and has difficulty with guessing. Adapting skills to new situations is problematic as home and school are completely different settings for Elizabeth and knowledge is not easily transferred.

12. Focus on detail and cannot distinguish between relevant and irrelevant details. Insists on copying each letter of the alphabet exactly and won't be swayed from such an activity. At school, Elizabeth appears to want to complete all the work set for her- she is often the last to line up to leave the classroom at lunchtime because she is finishing colouring in her workbook.

She sometimes finds it difficult to focus as she is sensitive to loud noise- pupils were cheering/clapping and she put her hands over her ears and said, "It hurts my ears." She wears her personalised headband and sometimes positions it over her eyes when she does not want to focus!

13. Cannot integrate factual information.
Elizabeth may know that it is sunny/hot but will put her coat, hat and gloves on.

14. An aspergers child cannot understand rules, their purpose and how they relate to them. Elizabeth is unable to remember a sequence- wash hands, then toilet. There may be an inability to focus on the immediate task/outcome- the child may know they are having a packed lunch but do not understand that it has to be packed and taken to school.

Some Key Problems For Elizabeth's Interaction Which May Relate To Your Own Child

1. The teaching of basic manners, aspergers children can have a problem with this- I teach my children the most important words, "Please" and "Thank you." However, my daughter does have her own added ritual where you say:
(a) "Please may I?"
(b) She receives what she has asked for and then says, "Thank you."
(c) You must then say, "You're welcome." If (c) does not occur she believes that you are being rude and will inform you that you have forgotten to say it. I then must say it. Fine at home; in the outside world, not always.

2. Behaving differently depending upon the situation- in school behaviour is more formal than at home. She does n't understand why it is so! Often children are unaware how to behave with others in certain situations and offending through personal comments is problematic.

This was perfectly illustrated to me when I was once in a secondary school and a year 9 aspergers boy looked straight at me and said, "Are you pregnant, Miss?" I was wearing a dress which I suppose was n't too flattering, that day. He did n't mean anything by it, he was n't being rude. I looked at him, laughed (all those teachers out there know the power of humour in the classroom which ensures that you stay sane) and said, "No, just fat today. I better not get a thing about my weight or you're to blame!" I knew him well and he and the small class laughed.

However, that same child once had to write about what upsets him and he said that he does not like it when he offends as he never means to do so- it just happens. There is a lack of control and people don't really like that powerlessness in real life.

3. Elizabeth won't pick up on social cues and once when I was crying she thought I was laughing and hit me in the face. Picking up on social cues does not come naturally and does have to be over-emphasised, somewhat! When Elizabeth's friend told the teacher that she was not being her friend, my daughter said that she thought it was a game that they were playing.

She can misread social cues. A male pupil tried to begin a friendly game with Elizabeth by continually shuffling towards her on his knees and smiling. She looked straight away and continued looking down at her workbook. In addition, Elizabeth continued tapping a child on the head; despite the pupil saying, "No," twice.

4. Understanding people and their roles in society- Elizabeth really needs to know who people are and we can't presume that she knows what others do/or indeed what their role entails. The Head teacher informed her class that he, "Looked after the school." She thought he cleaned/ tidied the school but had never seen him with a brush in his hand, so was confused. That is what looking after the school meant to her. Alex thought this was funny and tried to explain to Elizabeth- the situation improved when she began to have regular assemblies with the Head teacher.

When her class went to see a pantomime the Dame always chooses an audience member to terrorise- the Head teacher, in this case, had a Dame sitting on his knee. Elizabeth obviously did not understand the humour and asked if the person was his friend- why else would they be sitting on his knee? She told me that the Head teacher was happy for the friend to do this- she would have been upset/angry if he had not been and could not accept that the person was a stranger.

5. People who don't spend time/play with you don't necessarily dislike you (especially boys.) Elizabeth would not invite boys to her fifth birthday party- they seem to almost scare her and make too much noise. When she invited her girl friends some boys asked if they could come and she told them they were not invited. She began to draw pictures of her party and mentioned it a lot to people, drawing more attention to the fact she had not invited some.

6. If you upset someone and you apologise it helps and if you don't know how you have upset them you can ask. This is tricky, as you won't always understand their feelings but when she is older (hopefully) she will be able to accept that they are a person's feelings, nonetheless.

7. Telling the truth- at all costs my daughter will say things as they are (at home she will definitely vocalise, anywhere else she will believe it but not always say it out loud- luckily.) She

will tell her father that he smells and won't go near him (such things as smoking, not brushing your teeth.) She won't see it in herself, of course. So, not lying is problematic as she is brutally honest; the railway man once said, "She looks four years old, so no ticket." I forced him to sell me one as I know what she would tell the inspector, "I am five, not four!" She will tell me she does n't like a certain dress once I am wearing it and about to leave the house. When she compliments you it means a lot!

8. Learning to socialise- although she prefers her own company. I have watched Elizabeth initiate speech (finally she can now) but only rarely with people she knows/likes. With her peers she will repeat word-for-word obscure lines from films (usually quite silly ones, in a wide variety of voices/accents.) Often people won't understand but laugh at this stage. With adults she always asks them their name and tells them hers. So she has learnt how to have a basic conversation.

Before Elizabeth's fourth birthday, and lots of extensive speech therapy, she would say nothing to people- then they would ask her name; she would tell them and they could never understand what she was saying. They would ask again, she would shrug and skip off. Only later she began to get frustrated when people did not understand her. I would tell people her name and often explain my daughter briefly to them. Now, I feel she is more confident as she initiates a basic conversation. How it progresses is another matter - it is a start.

9. An asperger's child expects others to know their feelings- they can't understand why you don't know how they are feeling. They also cannot empathise- they think their thoughts are the way all feel and don't even realise that other people do think and feel. Elizabeth is frightened by the responses of others as she finds them unpredictable.

10. Little/no eye contact. Some children find this confrontational and Elizabeth avoids this at all costs!

11. For some aspergers children their tone of voice can be unusual- the same talk for adults and children. They may mimic others; Elizabeth does this with DVD character's voices. Speech can be formal and not always suited to the particular audience.

12. There can be a lack of the emotional awareness of anger/frustration. Elizabeth cannot see people are angry with her unless they shout; then she is inconsolable. She can be protective of pupils with whom she has as friendship. A friend was being reprimanded by another and Elizabeth frowned/looked really cross and moved to speak to her friend about it.

Learning Difficulties

Some children with aspergers can have more than one specific special need and in some cases it may be a learning difficulty; if you think of aspergers as being a difference then this helps to understand the distinction. I find two main problem areas with Elizabeth:

1. Comprehension in Literacy- this can be a problem as children cannot understand a character's thoughts and see inferred information. Elizabeth can tell me who the characters are in Snow White and Goldilocks and the Three Bears but cannot see that both female characters fell asleep in a stranger's house and they should not have. There may be a particular focus by the child on obscure detail; for example, Goldilocks broke a chair and that is, "Illegal," according to Elizabeth.

Recently, Elizabeth has had comprehension exercises from school as homework, based upon a book she is reading - she needs so much time to discuss every single detail. Her interpretation of situations often differs from the reality. At home we explain people/situations to our daughter but she needs clear instructions/guidance with lots of praise.

2. Aspergers children have a fixed imagination- they are unable to see the intentions of others and so are vulnerable. Elizabeth left school without me one afternoon and the teacher did not see her - she went to play on the swings with another child and her father.

In conclusion, I must admit, there have been so many times when Elizabeth has not been able to understand my viewpoint and so I have had to pause, smile and start anew the next day! In an ideal world I have the patience and the energy at all times; unfortunately, I am only human and it is the days when I can't make her understand which I find the hardest. I find this particularly difficult with regards to issues of safety as I have to take a firm stance- she is told what has to be so. She is vulnerable and needs to be protected so has to be aware of such issues as 'Stranger Danger' but not completely frightened by it all- in reality, the happy medium is not easy to reach!

PART TWO -

Elizabeth's Home/School Diary

Autumn Term - The Start of Something...

September 2008

Elizabeth has a lot of structure in her school day as I take, and collect her, from school; I have changed my job so I can do this- if she cannot see me from the window at the end of the day she is crying, "I thought I had lost you forever" and I have to go inside to collect her.

There is a problem with obsessive cleanliness and Elizabeth does not like to crease her clothes in school. She walks around lifting her pinafore up and I have to speak to her about not showing her underwear. She begins to take all of her school clothes off in school and her teacher asks me why she does this and I explain that she is concerned that they will be, "Messed up." I even have to put a towel over her clothes when having breakfast as she does not want any mess on them. At the end of a school day she will take them off incredibly carefully so as not to crease them.

Throughout this month Elizabeth really wants to have school dinners but her limited

language skills and repetition means that if she has choices she just repeats what people say; then has food that she does not like/has n't chosen. This worries me as I know she will not have eaten all day and will be upset. Finally, we decide to allow her to have school dinners; I have the menu and every day she is prepared for what she will eat, this works well.

However, not always. A typical example of what can happen with food choices occurred one day when she wanted meatballs and they had run out. She stood there rather confused whilst the welfare assistant explained this to her and then proceeded to list the alternatives. So many choices! Once she had finished she said, "Well then, Elizabeth, what would you like to eat?" To which, of course, she replied, "Meatballs!"

As there are problems with Elizabeth's language, the processing of information and her 'black and white' view of reality, what she tells me about school is difficult to understand. In fact, she refuses generally to talk about school as she is, "Home now." She is talking about a boy and becomes so frustrated with me because I do not know that he is a character in a book she has read at school!

October 2008

One day I decide to pick Alex up first. When I go to collect Elizabeth, the teaching assistant hands me her cardigan (as my daughter constantly leaves them on her peg in school) and I ask where she is. Panic sets in because she is not there. Eventually, I discover her playing on swings at a nearby school with her friend and her friend's father. The teacher comes to reprimand her and I speak to Elizabeth about the situation at home. She worryingly cannot see the danger. We punish her at home by sending her to bed early without any television. I ask her to repeat, "I should wait for Mummy, I don't run off." She gets the message and thankfully it does not happen again.

The Speech Therapist visits school to talk to the teaching assistant about strategies to use with Elizabeth to improve her language skills.

November 2008

The class are told that they will receive a book and related homework every week, Thursday in Elizabeth's case. She is accustomed to the library and her own books at home but easily becomes attached and does not like to give them back; at times, even sleeping with them! I'm glad she appears to be turning into a bookworm. I explain to her what the routine will be and Thursday morning she is prepared. That evening she suddenly starts searching for something around the house, when I ask her what she is doing she says, "I don't know if I should have changed my books," then she starts crying. It appeared that the books had not been changed.

I wrote a note to her teacher and the next day put it in the communication tray as she was busy with a child.

At the end of the day all the children leave without folders and I know that Elizabeth is going to 'blow' but I think that if I get her to the car then that will be damage limitation. However, she sees Alex's folder and runs back into class frantically sobbing, "I need my book." She can't find the folder so the teaching assistant tries to explain that they have not been changed but she is too upset; situations need to be off-set for her, explaining after-the-fact is pointless. Another teaching assistant gives Elizabeth the folder and she defiantly walks away (she does not want an audience when she is crying, but it does look rude.) I call her back because I know that unchecked, the school will have behaviour problems with her if she is allowed to walk off.

I finally get her to the car and she is sitting, stroking the book and saying, "You don't swap your book in that school anymore and it is mine now." I again write a note to her teacher who replies this time but misses the point of routine. I have to talk to the teacher about what actually happened and how unsettled/upset she was and am assured it will not happen again. Frustratingly for me that week it does, again.

Throughout the rest of the term sometimes the books are changed, sometimes not, or on the Friday. It appears that the routine is that there is no routine and I downplay the importance of the books/don't mention them at all, to my daughter.

Elizabeth begins to suck and put items in her mouth, I cannot leave her with certain toys so I have to take away her Polly Pockets until she stops. Every school day she continues to suck her school cardigan sleeve until it is soaking. At home she is very clingy, following me around and her sleep pattern becomes disrupted as she wets herself during the night.

Elizabeth constantly asks me about physical education, as she is concerned that she does not have it anymore at school. I mention it to her teacher and am told that this it is additional to outdoor play and that the school does not have to provide it in reception; but they do so from time-to-time. This does not help me, whatsoever. I am told that many of the children have been asking the same thing and that the class have been busy preparing for the carol concert and so have not had the time. This is understandable, but sitting the children down and explaining that would have been good practice for all, surely. I'm feeling frustrated by the lack of both structure and an understanding of Elizabeth's needs.

December 2008

There is some confusion concerning the Head teacher because Elizabeth thinks he is a visitor to the school as she does not see him every day. He tells the children that he takes care of the school and she tells me about this man, the caretaker! She says that he sweeps the floor with a broom- this is what she thinks it entails. Alex is laughing and she gets angry with him because he is laughing at her. Later, she is even more confused when she sees the Head teacher at mass on Sunday- why is n't he taking care of the school? I suppose it is quite logical!

It takes Elizabeth nearly two hours to write Christmas cards that she has personally selected for every pupil and staff member; she can remember about seventeen names. The next day I ask the teaching assistant for a class list, as I see her welcoming pupils. Her smiling, warm welcome to Elizabeth is always most appreciated. It frustrates me that communication, via the teacher, is relatively non-existent and the book for written communication does appear to not be working.

Elizabeth is diagnosed with aspergers by the paediatrician. On her return to school I inform her teacher of the diagnosis and she says that it must be mild because she appears to be no different to anyone else in the class. She tells me that Elizabeth's problems will start as she progresses through school as she has structure in reception. I do not expect people to under-stand my child fully, I am her mother and I certainly don't, but all I want is an awareness of her needs! Arghhh!

Spring Term- It Does Not Begin Well…

January 2009

The first week back and books are finally changed on the Friday! I sit Elizabeth down for fifteen minutes on Saturday afternoon and she does not want to look at these books as they, "Don't change them anymore," her usual repetition. I persist because I want her to focus and learn good habits and point out that they have been changed. I look through the book with her and she says, "Can I just draw the picture?" So I leave it at that. I write a note about the lack of routine and how Elizabeth has responded at home.

The teacher tells me that I am wrong to force my daughter to focus on anything. I think that she is nearly five years old and should be able to sit and concentrate at a table for ten minutes! I am aware that she wanders around her reception class and this is not helping her concentration one bit. Aspergers children need a focus and set routine or they do get 'lost' and can retreat into themselves- I am trying to make her less self-centred!

The new foundation stage has the onus on child-led activities for a child's emotional and social well-being. If your child is aspergers then this further compounds their difficulties! It also means that children do not receive adequate discipline and do learn to dictate their own learning. There are benefits as a child can develop their interests, but, I believe there has to be a time when you sit children down and they have to learn certain things that they may not, necessarily, want to. I teach children 1:1, in small groups and in whole classes and value inclusive teaching but I am unsure of the new foundation stage; however well-meaning it may be!

Elizabeth came back from school with her cardigan soaking from the shoulder to the wrist as she is sucking again and putting things in her mouth. The sleep situation continues to worsen and I feel like I have a newborn and not a child who will be five years old in the April. The bad dreams, also, become a concern. She dreams that I am in a blue hot air balloon, drifting off without her. She is sobbing uncontrollably during the night. My husband gets out of the bed to calm her down. She begins to try to tell him this dream so I get up. She is so concerned that I am going away in this balloon. When she calms down she asks me whether or not I would go without her. I have to reassure her that it was not real; it did not really happen, and was, indeed a dream. I did not go up in a hot air balloon and never intend to, and if I do then I would take her! I think I have all bases covered but she just wants to talk (no sleep) so she jumps into the bed and sleep comes as dawn breaks! Exhausting!

The bad dreams are always about people she cares about and who are central to her life. She wakes up crying because she has a dream that I am chasing her friend, wanting her to be my daughter. I know that when I collect the girls from ballet that I spend time with her friend but Elizabeth just needs reassurance that she is my child and that I love her.

It is the end of January and it is time for Elizabeth to no longer have the cot bed but to acquire a proper 'big girl' bed. I have already seen the perfect bed with a pink heart frame. So, I take her for a 'girly' shop, lunch and bed buying session. Of course, she loves the bed and we buy it. She is very withdrawn and won't sit on the bed when the shop assistant says that she can try it out. He, and his wife, are very kind to her but she clings to me. This is a common occurrence and I always explain to people that she does not socialise well with people.

This regularly happens with her ballet friend (who can be quite enthusiastic and likes to get right up close to you) greets her, Elizabeth's reaction is often just a look and a comment, "Don't shout." Watching the face of the other child fall is not good, as my daughter struggles with the noise and the physical proximity that the other child has in relation to her. I worry that she will struggle to make friends and offend people as she grows older.

The bed arrived a week later and Elizabeth was thrilled. We then had a 'girly' day in Liverpool- a hair cut, train ride, shopping, lunch and then to see Fifi at the theatre. I was offered seats in row B when I bought the tickets but asked for aisle seats on Q row- I must have been the only person who did not want the best seats in the house! The seats we had were good for her- if we sat too close then the noise would frighten her and the actual physical proximity could stress her. At the start of the production, there was thunder and lightning and she became really distressed by this, but I held her hand and explained that Fifi's garden was having a storm and that the noise would soon disappear. However, Stingo appeared and sprayed the front rows with a giant water gun. She cowered and began to cry- I had to tell her that he could not reach us. She calmed down when she realised that she was not wet. How happy I was for those seats in Q row!

February 2009

My husband and I attend a multi-agency meeting with my local authority advisory service, S.E.N.Co, teaching assistant, class teacher, A.S.D. Link Nurse and Speech Therapist; who is ill, so not present. Many items are discussed and further action (my local authority advisory service advise/give the class teacher support materials) is agreed upon. A few days later we have a Parents' Evening for my son, who is in year two, and the teacher mentions that he is showing signs of compulsiveness/routine. He sees what we automatically do for Elizabeth and thinks that certain behaviour is 'normal.' I have to explain to Alex how Elizabeth thinks/behaves is different to us and why we do what we do for her within our family.

It is important that I spend time just with Alex and we have always made time for this over the years. However, since they have both been at school it has become more difficult because I have to spend so much time with Elizabeth. He had previously had time with me straight after school before I would pick Elizabeth up from nursery and I think he misses that because now that they are both at school he does n't get so much 1:1 time.

So, it is mainly at the weekend and when Elizabeth goes to bed that Alex has more time with me. It has become harder to 'balance everything,' so to speak.

We start a new half term and the agreed communication with class teacher and teaching assistant, via the book, does not happen. Those first ten days in the new half term are problematic for Elizabeth. She refuses to eat certain foods at home and I discover that she is not eating at school, via my son and welfare assistants. The school had changed its menu and not informed parents. I have utter chaos as Elizabeth says that she does not know what the food is, so is not eating it. My son was of little help, as on two occasions he was unsure if he was eating chicken or fish. The dishes were different and there would be food that she would not be able to comprehend, i.e. fricasse and cobbler. So, I asked the office for a menu and they gave me the old one. Then there was more confusion as the welfare assistants said that it was given to the bursar, who said it was put in registers. Yet, still no-one can give me a copy. It is over three weeks before I receive the correct menu. I know that these things happen but it does not lessen the drama at home!

I also discovered (by pure chance, another parent) that Elizabeth's class had been allowed to go on the big playground at lunchtime and she was holding the welfare assistant's hand, not leaving her side. At home Elizabeth became more and more regimented as everything had to be in its place and I noticed that more toilet accidents were happening.

Elizabeth frequently cried at school and was unable to express why. A teaching assistant mentioned this in passing one day to me, thinking that it could be because I had not brought her to school that day, but her father. In fact, she cried for nearly an hour because her dad did not tie her hair into bunches! Sleep was becoming a problem again and I was tired and Elizabeth seemed to be forever fighting a cold (she is rarely ill.)

I was teaching 1:1 in various schools three times a week and had prepared her for this- she knew when her father was taking her to school and if I would be collecting her. She attended after school club twice a week this month with Alex and began to get into a routine.

March 2009

After two weeks at school I found eight pairs of knickers under Elizabeth's bed that did not belong to her, three so soiled that I threw them away. School had a record of one incident, but with several teaching assistants (one in the morning and one in the afternoon) supply teachers, class teacher and little communication between staff members, the number was obviously greater. As mentioned earlier, the written communication that had been promised did not happen during this two week period so I was left to discover facts from luncheon staff, other teaching assistants and friends.

Elizabeth began to continually talk about people not liking her and having no friends. Then one weekend she had a complete 'meltdown.' On the Sunday I found her upstairs hiding and in a state of panic as she had soiled herself and tried to hide it/tidy the mess; which in fact covered much of my bathroom, landing and stairs. What began as hiding, obviously turned to panic when she realised there was no escaping the mess.

When I discovered her she was sat on the toilet rocking herself, sobbing, "I should n't be doing this, they all think that I am a baby." This single image of my daughter is the one, despite all that we have been through, which saddens me the most. It became apparent that she knew she should n't be doing it, but when stressed, the toilet situation is always a problem. She thought all the other children were aware of her 'accidents,' when I don't think that this was the reality; it was her reality, nonetheless. I tried to reassure her and down-play the importance; we even spent some time talking through toilet urges which included me sitting on the toilet with her. This seemed to make her happier.

I went to the shops and bought her a back pack so any soiled underwear could be placed inside it (although I did stress it could merely be binned) so that she did not feel intimidated by walking out with a plastic bag with her soiled knickers inside, for all to see. I bought many spare knickers and left them in school. The doctor also gave her some laxative mixture to try one weekend but it caused her to have so much diarrhoea that she became very upset, so we stopped.

We build our daughter up so much confidence- wise and remain calm and reassuring; yet still have to deal with the fall-out of school. I was exhausted and rang in to work as I knew I had to take some unpaid leave to sort her out and talk to her teacher as I would have been in work early that morning and she would not have coped in school. Needless to say, I would n't have been able to function in work. What's more important? Elizabeth.

When Elizabeth went to school on the Monday I tried to explain to the teaching assistant but finally broke down, I had had enough of her reception year and was worried sick about my child; who had been awake most of that preceding night. It took this for the class teacher to actually speak to me and listen; communication improved somewhat, after this point. I went home and had a sleep.

Easter Holidays- April 2009

I spend time with Elizabeth on one of our 'girly' days and on the train to Liverpool she was rather disturbed by the noises of other people. She told me that her friend's daddy does not love her mummy anymore. Then, after much thought, she informs me that she will tell her friend this information on Monday! Hence, I have to talk to her about how she would feel in that situation- a long/hard battle but she eventually decides to not tell her friend.

The problem with friends/lack of was becoming her major topic of conversation. Young girls were beginning to say, "I'm not your friend," every five minutes, as they do. Elizabeth does take this literally and to heart and it confuses her. She thinks the boys are mean to her. I don't think that she is necessarily friendly towards them and mainly stays away, if she can. Hence, they are not always friendly towards her!

On the days (Easter holidays) leading up to her fifth birthday she makes me promise that I will play with her at her party, if no-one else will. Her party sees her mix, then when someone snatches the parcel from her during 'Pass the Parcel' she becomes so upset that she leaves the room. She plays, then sits and colours in by herself. There is a relatively small number of girls there as well. She complains about the noise, constantly; yet persists that she wants a party every year at the same play centre!

Summer Term- Waiting For An Improvement...

April 2009

Once Elizabeth returns to school the friendship concern is her major talking point; dreams and sleep again become problematic. She surrounds herself with more toys in school.

Then, the day I feared would come- Elizabeth wanted to be taken home and did not want to stay in school. After being upset one weekend it appeared on Monday morning that the previous Friday had seen a falling out with a friend which became physical- pinching and pulling hair. Her friend did not want to play with her and Elizabeth thought other girls were doing the same. She asked me to take her home, she did not want to stay. She clung to me for a while. I sat with her until 9.15 whilst she drew and I finally departed when she was distracted by a teacher and taken for a walk because I was going to look at a school who wanted me to work for them and I had to be there at ten o'clock.

I agreed to a part- time contract which allowed me to work from ten until two; it was a demanding job, I never left on time and was always rushing to Elizabeth's school. I brought work home and completed it when the children went to bed. It would suit the needs of my family, for the time being.

May 2009

At home we discuss friendship with Elizabeth and later her best friend, as well as the twin girls who are in her class, come to play after school. I spend some time observing the girl's interaction. I intervene about sharing and soon Elizabeth is playing the guitar and her friend singing as the girls are a 'band' with the twins dancing. I try to explain to the girls Elizabeth's ways and tell my daughter when she is being selfish and reward her for being a good friend (if only!)

I just seem to be getting her back on track when it is the long half term break and sleep becomes a real issue. She seems to be thinking all the time in bed and does not 'drop off' until at least 11 o'clock. I don't shout, just insist she gets back into bed. The only time that she mentions school is when referring to people not being her friend; every single day she says this.

June 2009

Elizabeth still, as always, has friendship issues. One Friday, I spend the evening with her, happily eating grapes and watching 'Beauty and the Beast;' after taking both children swimming in my gym. As usual, she does not mention school. The next morning she is calling me at five o'clock and comes into the bedroom talking about some boys; we think that she has had a bad dream. She asks me if this boy knows where she lives and I say that he does not. However, she finally tells me that a boy in her class has said that he will discover where she lives, get her toys and chop their heads off (she sees these toys as her friends!) She then asks me what I will do if this boy knocks at our door and it takes a long time- day out in Formby, including lunch, before she calms down about this boy.

Then, she tells me about another boy who constantly draws over her drawings and I tell her that she must tell the teacher as these boys have to be shown how to behave, they are not bad (obviously she is not convinced!)

We take her to the family night at school and she plays with a friend, to begin with, and then by herself. She seems a little more settled but awakens at five the next morning, sobbing, as she has completely wet the bed; I change her and put her in our bed as her own bed is soaking. The next morning she does not want to go out at all so I don't take her to mass (only Alex) and she plays in the garden and completes jigsaws with her dad.

I speak to the teaching assistant on the Monday as the class teacher is on a course. The children concerned are spoken to at school but it happens again. On the Tuesday one child threatens to harm her toy crab and she tells a friend, not the teacher. When I ask her why she does not tell a teacher she says, "I like children who are nice to me," over and over again. I leave her be and later her father speaks to her about it.

We both find that the processing of information and the communication of our daughter to others is a real problem; even more so, right now. We are aware that she does not have another Speech Therapist, at present, and do not know how that is going at school as there is still little communication, via the book. However, I am still following the Speech Therapy course with her at home.

A couple of days later the other boy who draws over her drawings, runs up to her with a water bomb (in front of me, his mother is obliviously walking so far ahead) and Elizabeth physically cowers. I know that she is becoming a target, as a vulnerable child. I attend the class trip on the Friday as Elizabeth wants me to be there, in case no one else sits by her. I can see how young and fragile she looks compared to other children in her class. I can also see the dreadful behaviour of the two boys whom she has problems with.

That weekend, Elizabeth is up during the night, then put back to bed. On the Sunday she is tired and has a tummy upset/diarrhoea; she eats little all day and develops a temperature. She is up that night with toilet issues and in the morning tells me that she feels a little sick and does not want to go to school. When I ask her why she says that the boys hate her and are mean, her girlfriends won't let her play with others and won't always play with her. She is a bit brighter when Alex promises to play with her the next day in school; he has his own friends/ life, though. We decide to let her rest at home but make it clear that she will be in school the next day. My husband takes the day off work as annual leave to be with her.

July 2009

There is a lack of routine towards the end of a term and party time. One day Elizabeth's class went into the hall for a special assembly. The boy who had previously threatened her toys was sitting by the teacher as he was in need of teacher guidance! In the morning, whilst they were walking into the room, he hit Elizabeth and her brother (who was already in the room) saw him. The teacher did not see this.

In the afternoon Elizabeth was in class and the boy hit her again- her friend told the teaching assistant and the boy was reprimanded. All of this time the boy's parents are unaware of the problem he has with my daughter as school/teacher has not spoken to them about it. Why? I don't know!

When I pick Elizabeth up from school she is very upset. As we are walking out of school Alex tells me what happened in school- he is angry and I talk to him because I don't want him to retaliate on his sister's behalf. She then tells me that he was reprimanded in the afternoon because he hit her again. I had no choice but to approach the parent and just then I saw the mother walking towards me. I stopped her and told her what had happened. She said that he could n't have, he knows not to hit girls. However, I said he had done so, twice that day. The boy then admitted he had and the astonished mother said, "Well, you don't hit girls, no matter what they do to you!"

At this point I told her that Elizabeth has aspergers, she stays away from boys, she does n't go anywhere near him as she feels threatened. I then told her what he previously had done (i.e. "I'll find out where you live..") I do believe that she sniggered/laughed- at this point! I said that the school is aware of Elizabeth's problems, are helping with our family and as a result of what he did the reality is my daughter was upset. I was shocked by her lack of understanding but I now expect her son to keep his hands to himself!

The next day I told the teacher all about what had happened and explained that I do not want to be called into school because my son retaliates if he sees this happening again. It is near the end of term so the teacher said that details will be passed on to the next teacher- would a talk with both of the boy's parents have hurt? I have to become this parent who feels that she is constantly harassing the teacher and she is constantly defensive and this makes talk difficult. I stress what has been happening, just state the facts but I am constantly made to feel that I am bothering her. I don't do it every day, just when it is essential for Elizabeth's welfare.

This has been a stressful school year for our family and I am overjoyed that it is ending. My daughter knows her new teacher but there is a problem- she is having a baby and it is due in September. I have known this for some time and have told Elizabeth that this lady will not be her teacher for the beginning of year one, but after the Christmas. For a while it was uncertain who would be her next teacher so I did not mention it to Elizabeth until the school announced who that teacher would be. Thankfully, it is a supply teacher who she knows (and likes) so it is discussed at home and school with Elizabeth on a regular basis. She also has a photograph of the supply teacher which she looks at to remind her.

I have changed my own job this academic year and been more flexible and if I had not I know that Elizabeth would not have coped as well as she has. I have been on hand to take her to school most days and collect her, except for a few occasions when she attended after school club with her brother and my husband has done the morning run.

I did initially think that the new foundation stage for children would be good for her as the focus is really on emotional and social well-being. However, there is a lot of unstructured time and a child-centred learning focus- this sounds good but for an aspergers child it does create confusion when there are not clear routines/boundaries; for a child who is ultimately self-centred in the first place, it can make their socialisation very difficult. In life children have to sit down and concentrate on tasks that are not of their own desire and if we delay that then behaviour in our classrooms will suffer.

Summer Holidays 2009

The school Summer holidays are always the most difficult for an aspergers child as there is such a long break in routine. I have to establish some routine over the next six weeks as it can appear to be such a void, endless mass in the child's mind eye. Every night before bed I speak to Elizabeth concerning the events of the next day, always with the main focus of the day- be it the cinema, play centre, visiting the grandparents.

Obviously, the main event will be the Summer holiday and this year we are taking the children to The Portaventura Theme Park in Spain. Elizabeth loves her home and so time spent away from it can upset her. When we go away on holiday she has to be shown lots of photographs of where we will be staying and places we will be visiting. She now knows that she will be staying at a 'holiday home.' She packs her various toys and clothes in her own suitcase. Whilst we are away she is fine so long as she knows what is happening; today's main activity- theme park, city visit, walk, play centre or swim. A clear order of events is needed at all times.

The end of August is problematic as she will be returning to school at the start of September. As the beginning of term encroaches Elizabeth has already began to question Alex's liking of school, "I just don't get it, Alex, why do you like it so much?" She does not want to return. I invite friends to play from school so she is socialising and one day I invite a house full of children- like a mini school.

Autumn Term- Here We Go Again…

September 2009- Year 1

This is always a tricky month for aspergers children as it is a major routine change. It begins as well as can be expected. I note that the boy whom Elizabeth had problems with last school year is placed on the same table as her so I know that the details have not been passed on to the new teacher. Then she receives her first written homework and it is difficult to get her to write on lined paper and form her letters in a certain manner. I try to show her but she just sits and cries because she says that she has completed her homework, "Wrong." She has it in her head what is right and does not like being shown differently. Her aspergers does make her see things through her own eyes and I am eager that she is corrected now or she will learn incorrectly. Needless to say, I will have many tears/sulks to come.

Hence, I inform the teacher that she will need to be firmly cajoled or she will just do what she wants to do and then you will never get her to do anything you want her to! This is one of my fears for her education from now on. I am also aware that I spend so much time working on social situations with her that the more academic side is underdeveloped. She learnt hardly any sounds last school year (I only did some with her) and the reading does not 'knit together' as it should, as a result. Elizabeth does become disheartened and upset if she feels she cannot do something and she says, "They expect me to read in that school and I can't." She so wants to be independent. I feel bad that I haven't done enough.

I am unsure of the new foundation stage, as you can remember, and believe that if the government want children to be independent readers by the age of seven then this is not the correct way to achieve such goals.

In addition, when I begin to focus upon sounds Elizabeth does not see this as correct saying, "You don't do that! We don't do that in school." It is early September and I inform her that the new teacher will be covering this work. Those with aspergers need the system to be regimented in a particular manner from the outset and I have seen so many changes in education over the years and this one has not been in Elizabeth's favour.

Two weeks into the term and Elizabeth has not been sleeping well for many nights so her eyes look a little sore; the doctor gives me eye drops. The nightmares begin again- screaming at 3.30am and not returning to sleep. She is also having many toilet issues. She does seem more settled, though, believe it or not!

Elizabeth is n't always good with people but does seem to like animals. So, we consider horse-riding lessons. We first visit the stables and I am impressed by the staff's interaction with her. I inform the staff at Bowlers all about her. She attends every Saturday or Sunday, whenever I can get a lesson; this place is so fantastic that there is a waiting list. Then one day she fell off the horse and banged her arm- they encouraged her to get back on, though, and we were so proud of her.

October 2009

Elizabeth seems to be quite a different child- she is making many new friends at school and we are so pleased. She even begins to say, "Hello!" to some boys on her arrival at school. One day she comes running out of school telling all about a little boy. Her class were on their way to the computer room and this boy, apparently, opened the door for her so she kissed him on the cheek. They sat together at lunch holding hands.

The very next morning she sat down next to the same boy and held his hand. This boy is a really gentle little boy and she later became friends with another similar boy and attended the birthday parties of both- she does n't usually want to go to such parties! She does not really associate with the boys who are just typical boys- they are often too loud and frighten her. She only talks to a few of my son's friends because she says that they have evil faces!

However, she did begin to tell me that boys are nice to you if you kiss them- just like when she became friends with the first boy. I had to explain to her that you don't have to kiss all the boys in order to be their friends! She does not know how to start a conversation- she finds it 'hit and miss;' so she thought that had worked well so I'll try it again. It worked well in that particular situation but I did say that not everyone likes to be kissed; she did n't really understand why as she likes a kiss!

November 2009

Elizabeth has been very 'clingy' with me and I have had to focus her on school. She has been complaining that school 'stinks of poo.' I know it is silly but she has asked me if she can leave school! She is a bit over-sensitive on the senses side, anyhow!

After the half-term holidays she did n't want to go back to school and had been asking about the weekend from Wednesday morning- "Is it the weekend today?" I have told her that I have to work and that all little girls have to go to school or the policeman will arrest their parents. She does understand but has spent the week wanting to be just with me.

Also, after half-term the class get additional homework- the dreaded spellings and Elizabeth cannot hardly read any of the words. In addition, she does not know so many sounds and the reading is not 'knitting together,' as it should. I ask if she can complete the spellings out of class with the teaching assistant when the other children have their spelling test. She is also beginning to write her letters backwards.

Elizabeth could not complete her homework sheet that was all about telling the time. She could not recognise the number 7, let alone tell me that it was 7 o'clock; she also did not know 12 and she is doing the same with letters of the alphabet. When reading she is still not really breaking down words, down, she could n't even read the first letter but thought that it was b. I am helping her in short bursts with lots of patience/support/praise and lots of literacy teaching to reinforce what school are doing. Elizabeth loves this teacher and the teaching assistant.

I report to school that we are having a bad time with Elizabeth at home and getting her into school becomes problematic. She has become frustrated, tearful and quite aggressive. She does not like leaving me in the morning and I always have to go into the classroom and hang around as she sometimes follows me outside. She begins to realise that if she does not enter the classroom then I cannot leave.

On the worst day, it takes me ten minutes to get her into the classroom and then she just cries and turns her back to the teacher. She just blocks everyone out and nobody can console her, not even her best friend. The teaching assistant says that I can stay at the side and there is a supply teacher. The S.E.N.Co comes out and looks at the situation- by now Elizabeth is beyond controlling her emotions. The S.E.N.Co takes her for a walk and after half an hour I scurry off to work. When I collect her from school she runs out and pushes her forehead against mine shouting, "I missed you, I missed you!" She is so angry that I left her and I have to push her away from me as she is pushing so hard that she is hurting my head.

My husband bought tickets for Elizabeth and I to attend 'The Disney Princess on Ice' show at The Echo Arena in Liverpool. We travelled by train and she dressed as Ariel and had her photograph taken with a statue of the real Ariel in the foyer. She loved the show- there was so much space. Then we walked into Liverpool, had lunch and a quick shop. It was lovely to see Elizabeth enjoying herself doing normal 'girly' things.

December 2009

Elizabeth comes home from school talking about wearing pyjamas for school. The next day she says that she has to wear her pyjamas for school that day. I say that she does not, the teacher would have told/sent a letter to all parents. When I arrive at school I ask the teacher what Elizabeth is talking about and she says that for the school play, in three weeks time, children will be wearing their pyjamas and will also need a soft toy and blanket. She won't let her belongings stay at school so I have to buy some new pyjamas, a blanket and a bear. I place them in a bag and leave them at school - these can all be used in school for the various rehearsals and performances.

The school is not working to timetable at the moment and Elizabeth is reading Mr Men books and sounding out lots of words. Performance rehearsals are taking up a lot of the day. The teacher and the teaching assistant help to keep her focused. I try to encourage her to take a toy in for 'Golden Time' (this is every Friday when the children can bring in their own toy and play with it for a set amount of time in the afternoon.) Elizabeth has never wanted to as she would have to put the toy in a box and it is dark in there and she cannot see her toy. This would stress her all day! So, she would rather be without the toy.

Christmas Holidays

Elizabeth had a great holiday but it will be difficult to get her back into school. She woke up screaming one night at 4.30am because she dreamt that she was at school and there were ghosts and strangers; a hen was also pecking her, "To death." She has told me that school should n't allow hens in school (I'm sure the Head teacher does not, I have assured her.)

She has been questioning Alex about how long she has to stay at school and said to him, "I don't understand why you like it so much." School should not take it personally, she would just rather do what she wants. She also likes the familiar home setting and has been my shadow all holiday. So, days before school commences I have to stress that it will begin soon; without it being too much of a countdown and holiday spoiler!

Spring Term- Full Of Optimism…

January 2010

The New Year begins with so much snow! At the end of the first day back to school the Head teacher decides to close, just for the next day. It really confuses her and she now thinks that it is the weekend. Elizabeth wets and soils herself a lot that first week- at home I have to continually remind her to go to the toilet. On the first Friday back I walk home with the children and as soon as we reach home I change their wet clothes (snow), bathe them and put both children into their pyjamas. When Elizabeth took her clothes off it became clear that she had soiled herself and tried to wipe it but made it worse- from the tops of her legs, right up her back, there was poo! I threw the knickers away and bathed her.

She said that she was in school talking to her friend and soiled herself- I don't know what time it was. Her Dad and I both questioned her about this and she finally said that it takes too long. We stressed that she must go because she often smells when she gets home (she wets herself and says that it is okay because it has dried.)

I use a toilet picture card positioned in the house to remind her all weekend and she picks it up when she wants to make a visit! I also have set times when she goes. It does not seem a priority (in her mind) but should be a routine for her. I tell school to be careful if she feigns illness. She pretended to be ill one Friday with a sore tummy (not the first time) and said that she would have to stay home with me. However, five minutes later I caught her jumping up and down on our bed. At school they set up a system where the teaching assistant reminds her about going to the toilet up until lunch and then the class teacher does so in the afternoon.

Elizabeth begins to have incomplete work- a handwriting scheme booklet needs completing so we take it home. It seems that she is taking so long colouring in every detail of the pictures. We work on it every weekend until it is completed. I am also working on lots of booklets provided by Autism Initiatives and constantly use a visual timetable with her at home (see part 3 for more information.)

February 2010

Elizabeth seems to be going from strength- to- strength! She has just achieved level two swimming- which included two lengths of the children's swimming pool at the sports centre where she has her lessons. She has always had her lessons in a class of three but lately the numbers have increased but she seems to be okay because it is mainly girls and they are rather quiet. She commented on the lack of space, however, when she received a kick to her head. I will have to monitor the situation as it has taken her so long to settle with an instructor and generally she wants to please and tries to remain focused- rather different than when she first began lessons, and many instructors later.

The Speech Therapist visited school to asses Elizabeth and sent a report showing an immense improvement. I compared it to all of her others since the age of three; she was really weak in this area and we have worked hard on it at home/school. I feel that all the hard work is finally reaping some rewards. However, they sent me facial expression work- this area has improved but continues to be one of her weakest areas as she cannot distinguish people's emotions. I have already completed the facial expression booklet that I am sent with Elizabeth twice before- we will try again as she may be at the right stage to internalise the content this time around.

At February half-term she knows (as always) what she is doing every day and the family visit Chester for a long weekend. She knows where we are staying (via the hotel's website) and the itinerary of events whilst there- shopping, hotel, meal. Next day- walk around the wall, boat ride, a swim at the hotel and then dinner in Chester at an Italian restaurant where she can share a large pizza with her brother and have some orange juice. She sits with her brother giggling at the end of the evening in the hotel room- she has loved her day!

What is different is that when she returns to school she is eager to talk about her holiday with the teaching assistant. Elizabeth has a lot of activities which happen every weekend but will she talk about them? No. When I ask her, or tell her that I will tell the teaching assistant, she will ask me not to as she does not want them to know; I think she often expects them to already do so.

March 2010

I have been thinking about how different this March is from last year. Elizabeth is so much more settled- when she arrives at school she sits down and has a book that she draws in; this structure makes it easier for me to leave and has a calming influence upon her. She still draws the same thing every day- her two goldfish, Spongebob and Squidward. No matter where she has been, she does not draw about it. She has been to a party one weekend so on Monday I say, "Are you going to tell the teaching assistant all about it?" However, she replies, "No, don't tell her, it's not school." Sometimes she will tell; if encouraged by others, especially when questioned.

The two goldfish die one day. She returns from school and immediately notices so I tell her that they have a tummy ache; just like when she is sick, they don't move. I buy new fish. When she is older I will tell her the truth, on this occasion it did not hurt anyone!

The temporary teacher leaves and Elizabeth has been prepared for the arrival of the teacher she remembers, from when Alex was in that class. The teacher visits school first, so that helps and so does the photograph that I have with all of the other visual material that I use. She begins to draw something new in the morning- her previous teacher whom she liked so much. She is impressed by the new teacher and becomes good at tidying up in school- something she mentions constantly because she did it so well. She decides to bring in a water bottle like her friends- something that I have always encouraged but which she did not want to do. She also brings a toy into school for 'Golden Time' and places it in the box so it can 'play with the other toys!?'

It is time to book Elizabeth's birthday party and she wants it in the same place as the previous two years! Will she invite boys? Yes, the same two whom she likes in her class. Major breakthrough. She receives an invite to another party (twin boys) and does not want to go to their party so I don't force the issue. She likes particular people and associates with them but outside school she is even more particular of who she mixes with!

I have noticed that my daughter is becoming very protective of her friends- if someone tries to hurt/shout at anyone she cares for (especially her close girlfriends) then she becomes so angry and wants to comfort them- this is really another breakthrough for her. Empathy! We spend a lot of time on this skill- maybe it is beginning to bear fruit, so to speak! She also begins to really dislike unkind behaviour and becomes friendly with another boy she rarely speaks to because someone hurt him. She cannot understand the unkind boy.

I buy a new car- the same make, model and colour as I always do because Elizabeth is very attached to the car she calls, "Yo-Yo the Yaris." She does notice every minute detail in which it differs from the last car, though. However, she is fine with the change! I remember when my husband and I part-exchanged our vacuum cleaner for another model- she cried and complained for days.

Easter Holidays 2010

We are going on holiday to Paphos, Cyprus, and Elizabeth has packed her own Bratz suitcase. She is prepared for the holiday village as she has seen all the pictures, via the website. She knows the order of events each day and loves the splash pool, adventure park and walking along the beach.

Back in England the holidays are structured for her. One day we go to a play centre where all the girls and mums meet up. Elizabeth's friend says, "I am not your friend" and she sobs. When I take her home she tells me that her friend won't let her play with anyone else and she wants to. I tell her that it is fine to play with lots of different people. She asks if she is allowed and I say that she is. I say that she should still play with her 'old friends' as well - all girls together. I am pleased that she is finally playing with more children but know that this whole area is a minefield for her! It's natural for girls to constantly fall out but she does not understand why and cannot read from facial expressions and gesture if someone is unhappy with her. Not easy!

So, Elizabeth will be six years old this month- I have covered her life from 0-5 and leave her story incomplete…My major concerns for her are, obviously friendships, but also what she understands and the discrepancy between that and what people actually think she does! The best example of what I mean is the fact that Elizabeth has never understood that Jesus was born at Christmas (she thinks he died then) and is, in fact, supposed to be the baby in the crib during her nativity plays. She also attends mass nearly every week and sees visual representations of the nativity. However, at the time that this book goes to press I have finally discovered why she thinks so. The lack of snow at a nativity scene. It cannot be Christmas. So, I have explained to her a little about the weather in The Middle East…

PART THREE -

Advice/Help For Parents And Carers

Problems Associated With A Diagnosis

The time before a medical diagnosis can be uncertain, stressful and the whole process seems to take forever! Your child will be referred to several specialists who are in demand (so you have to wait) but it is important to receive the correct diagnosis; so more than one visit to a paediatrician is necessary. Each aspergers child is different so your child may not instantly fall into a category- hence, the need for further investigation.

Some families don't want to label their child because of the negative stigma attached to having a special need. Once you have a label- what then? I have seen some children receive a diagnosis and neither the family nor the child have been ready/prepared or given appropriate guidance. In my experience, the older a child is, the worse this has been. In the secondary sector the condition should have been noted by various professionals during the primary stage. A major problem is that training/awareness greatly differs from school to school and Local Education Authority.

I have worked in schools with suicidal teenagers because they have had a diagnosis and think of this condition as a disease, from which they cannot escape. Many have already had years of feeling different, uncertain and stressed in life. Then, they are left with the diagnosis and many unanswered questions.

The parents involved are unsure what to do next. One parent told me that she did not want to put in place a few suggestions that I had made because she did not want her child to feel different and for others to see him as so. However, he was different, he had known for some time and so had other people- with some explanation for his behaviour people would be more understanding and could help.

By not putting strategies in place to help and accessing various services this parent would not be helping her child. This was all because she had not been given any professional guidance and did not even know what aspergers was. She had a talk with me where I spoke to her about aspergers and she held my hand and cried- her son was 14 years of age. The whole system simply let that family down and that both angers and upsets me.

What is important is that the child receives help as soon as possible and a diagnosis is needed these days to get such support- many will say that you can get access to services before/without a diagnosis but I found it difficult getting the correct help and my daughter had a diagnosis at the age of four!

Some parents may feel shock/anger/blame and bereavement for the child that has been lost. Then comes the realisation that he/she will have this condition forever. Try to be the ultimate optimist and learn to accept it all at your own pace. Remember that you know your child best. Sometimes it can feel like it is too much. You may experience negative thoughts towards your child and think about, "What if?"- don't, as your child wouldn't be who they are if they were different.

You may feel alone/isolated and that you have to explain your child's actions to people- I have done this when there have been those who have questioned Elizabeth's behaviour. People can see your child's behaviour as 'odd'- and this can show in their very manner and they may even vocalise this to you. They may try to offer their own experience/opinion of rearing a child without any awareness of your situation. Just tell them that your child is aspergers (some parents give strangers a card which explains the condition)- that is why they behave so; I have found that tends to silence people because they have an explanation or don't understand what you are talking about!

It helps to speak to friends and parents of children who are aspergers for support and there are many parent support groups in existence. My Local Educational Authority has a magazine that is sent to me which details such assistance. A.S.D. Link Nurses are also 'worth their weight in gold' at this stage and your doctor can put you in touch with these.

General Advice To Parents Of Children With Aspergers

As a parent you must believe that:

1. It is not your fault! I blamed myself, thinking that I could have done more to help Elizabeth when she was younger. I now don't think about blame- it's wasted energy.

2. It is not an illness- your child has not got a disease and there is nothing 'wrong' with them- they merely have different needs. My child is aspergers, she does not have aspergers- it is not a disease. A label has a tendency to emphasise the negative, not the positive and the person.

3. You can use your child's interests to their advantage and nurture them. There are many differences in people and these are to be celebrated, not denied, nor changed. Aspergers children have a strong ability to focus/concentrate and are good at learning facts- 'word for word.'

4. Don't take anything for granted- human beings learn to communicate innately (instinct, without thinking) but your child will have to learn what others take for granted. Never assume!

5. Your child will not be 'cured' - I avoid reading anything that tells me so! Do approach the internet with caution, look at reputable, knowledgeable websites only. Contact The National Autistic Society (N.A.S.) helpline on 0845 070 4004 or look at autismhelpline@nas.org.uk

6. You have to modify life to help your child. I have met many parents who have not accepted this because they don't want their child to feel different. The reality is that your child has always felt this way. It can be a relief or a shock; accepting it means that you can then seek help and your child will benefit.

7. Take some time for yourself, time to adjust- it can be a great healer. Remember: you know your child best so don't be pushed into anything by those who think they know best. Life does improve, honest!

8. Children do often grow up to marry, have children and a career. For many, it is all about learning to cope.

9. You should feel free to discuss any concerns at school or nursery. Visit your doctor and ask for an assessment/ diagnosis through a referral to a Community Paediatrician or Educational Psychologist. Take action/control- empower yourself with information.

10. PULL- Patience, Understanding, Love and Laughter... they all work for me!

Before Formal Schooling Begins

·   There should be an enhanced school transition meeting where all professionals involved with the child (such as nursery workers, Pre-School S.E.N.Co, Local Education Authority officials, Health Visitor, Speech Therapist, A.S.D. Link Nurse, parents and school) talk about the needs of the child in the school setting.

·   Reciprocal visits (two is enough, at different times of the day) to school should be arranged in the Summer term before school entry; the child should wear school uniform for these.

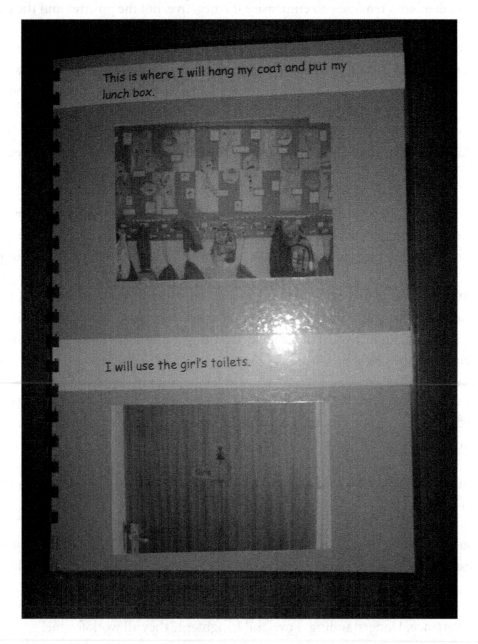

·   An album of photographs showing new people and the school environment should be compiled; nursery took Elizabeth there and did it all.

·   Visual sequences to support the child's independence should be used, e.g. Elizabeth hanging up her coat on the peg and putting the lunchbox in the appropriate place.

·   Dressing skills need attention. There can be different Summer/Winter uniforms in operation and also a Physical Education uniform to consider. Children have to be familiar with each and know when they are to be used.

Educational Provision

What is the right type of school?

The alternatives:
Either:

A mainstream school where support or resources base is provided, dependent/suited to the child.

Or:
Special school-expertise.

Remember- once your child is at school:

·   The curriculum should be adapted to meet your child's needs- do they have an Individual Education Plan?

·   Is the school an appropriate environment? Keep a diary of what triggers your child's frustration/stress; learn to see how it shows itself, for example walking/climbing on furniture and throwing items.

·   Monitor the level of 1:1 support from a skilled professional. Do you feel that you can approach school as soon as a problem arises?

·   Are school and parents working together/discussing issues/supporting the child. Do you need regular termly meetings with the S.E.N.Co/class teacher?

·   Do all the staff understand aspergers?

·   Is/has staff training available/been completed?

·   Be aware of the S.E.N. system- there are various categories.

The S.E.N. System- Made Simple

This is a 3 stage model:

1. School (or early years) Action- the school acknowledges that the child has a particular need but is able to provide the special educational provision that may be needed.

2. School (or early years) Action Plus- outside agencies may become involved, such as L.E.A. support workers, speech therapists, Autism Initiatives and so on…

This is the stage that Elizabeth should be placed.

3. Statementing- if your child isn't making any progress under stages 1 and 2 and needs more extra help then the L.E.A. may issue a statement which will detail the additional help needed; funding may be allocated accordingly.

Some authorities have an additional School Action Plus Intensive stage which is especially for those with real medical need who often need a helper.

An Individual Education Plan

This is a planning document for a pupil at the school action and above stage, in line with the S.E.N. Code of Practice. It identifies a child's immediate social/learning needs and details any other special arrangements which should be made to suit the individual. It describes the arrangements made to monitor and review progress and to ensure the child's entitlement is met. Resources needed are specified on the I.E.P.

The Principle Of I.E.P.s

Focus on collaborative educational effort - a number of people are helped to work together towards the educational goals for one child.

An I.E.P. should be flexible but will:

Be brief and action based.

Indicate the pupil's current level of achievement.

Identify the nature, extent and specific areas of a pupil's social/learning difficulty.

Specify a program and set specific relevant targets to be achieved against criteria which acknowledge success and represent achievable goals.

Detail any other additional support or resources.

Indicate how carers/parents will be involved and what support or encouragement is being provided.

Include, if appropriate, contributions from the pupil and their views on their social/learning needs.

Set clear monitoring and recording arrangements, with dates.

Be reviewed at least once a year. Parents should always receive a copy.

Targets should be:

Specific
Measurable
Achievable
Relevant
Timed

An example of the layout of a school I.E.P. :

ndividual Education Plan- Any School

Pupil:		D.O.B/ School year	Stage:	School Action +	Description of need:	Aspergers and atten- tion difficulties.

Start Date	Targets	Resources/Intervention and Strategies	End Date	Outcomes/Future need
	To follow instructions with 2 and 3 key words. To develop an under- standing of positional language: below, above and so on.	Speech and Language pro- gram to be followed daily with a Teaching Assistant.		Achieved. Speech and Language as- sessment needed.
	To understand and adhere to the 'good sitting/listening and looking' prompts.	All staff at appropri- ate times. Ask the child questions to check understanding.		To continue target to ensure it is embedded and to start to not rely upon prompts. Continue to use a visual timetable and introduce a task organiser, such as an egg timer, to show how much time is left.
	To know the structure of the school day.	Visual timetable.		To avoid stressful situa- tions by knowing the school routines- ongoing.
	The development of the child's abil- ity to communicate their emotional and physical needs; when upset and within different situations.	Teacher and Teaching Assistant to encourage the child to talk when they be- come upset.		To be able to communicate needs verbally- continue. Introduce 'Comic Strip Conversations' with Teaching Assistant, on occasions when the child is upset.

To focus upon tasks without distractions.	To leave objects from home on the table in the class before story time.	Objects/toys did not distract the child from their work.
To develop social skills/concepts and to recognise emotions. To improve understanding of social parameters of relationships, friendships and increase emotional awareness.	Through the use of stories, puppets and scenarios within small groups. To discuss appropriate behaviours.	To recognise feelings and communicate these with others in an appropriate manner- ongoing. To introduce Socialisation In Practice Sessions- through OSSME; to be followed once a week by a Teaching Assistant. To have a wider range of friends and a better understanding of relationships and emotions.
Ensure that the child is included in whole class instruction.	To use the child's name to focus attention and minimise language- ask questions to check for understanding.	To understand her place in the class- ongoing.

47

Remember...

If you have concerns about the service your Local Educational Authority is providing for your child contact your local Parent Partnership Service. They advise/support parents whose children have special educational needs. There may be gaps in professionals' understanding but try to remain calm and accept that the system is not perfect- difficult, I know, when as a parent/carer you are concerned about your child!

At What Age Do You Tell Your Child About Their Aspergers?

This is a difficult area and depends upon the child. Some children know that they are aspergers without really knowing what it entails- they do have a general idea but not the 'whole picture,' so to speak. I would try to encourage this as long as you can. I believe that when Elizabeth is in year 8 (roughly twelve years old) that it would be a good time. Starting a secondary school in year 7 will be stressful so I want her to settle. I want to address issues as they arise- she may come to question and know certain things earlier but the 'full picture' needs time and I want her to be at an age when she is mature enough. She is a child- five years old now and I want her to enjoy her childhood without the analysis. I simply think it may be too overwhelming for her when she is at primary school.

There can be problems with leaving it too late to tell- but these depend upon the child. I have seen a 14 year old boy who had previously been suicidal be suddenly diagnosed with aspergers For years he had known he was different but did not know why.

A girl I knew at sixth form level was told at the age of 16; gradually taught about her differences and what they meant to her. She was not overwhelmed but 'drip feed' information so that she could absorb it and said, "It now all makes sense." A boy had called her, "Weirdo," when she was in year 10 at school- she had never forgotten that. I think she should have been told earlier.

Communication Difficulties That May Affect Individuals with Aspergers

·   May not understand the purpose of communication and not listen to others.
·   May not show/share interest. Problems with the give and take of communication.
Speech may be delayed/extra time may be needed for language to be processed.
·   May have a good vocabulary, speak fluently; yet struggle to communicate/ understand.
Signing- this can assist speech. I used this when Elizabeth's language was poor. I took a year course and acquired a British Sign Language Level 1 qualification.

How to Support Communication

·   Address the individual by their name and ensure that they know you are talking to them.

·   Give time for communication to be processed and do not use too many words.

·   Explain jokes, metaphors/idioms.

·   Try to understand their frustration.

Sensory- The Importance Of Sight, Sound, Touch, Taste and Smell To An Aspergers Child.

Sound/Noise

·   Don't have too much noise- switch off the television if you want to talk. Use calming background music. Use earphones and block out sounds.

·   Provide a warning of loud noises and a quiet place, if needed. Let the child indicate when they cannot cope.

·   Get the child's attention before you give instructions and use actions when you want them to listen. They may not be able to look and listen at the same time. Only have one person speaking at a time. Vary your tone of voice when speaking to the child.

·   Children can be particularly over-sensitive to noise which is not of their own making. For example, Elizabeth can beat on a drum and the noise won't bother her but at school when her friends were cheering/clapping she put her hands over her ears and said, "It hurts my ears." Be aware of this!

Visual

·   Sensitivity to changes in light/dislike of bright sunlight. Elizabeth has problems concentrating in certain light. Use sunglasses or a shaded area.

·   Children can be fixated on what they see and Elizabeth, for example, will recognise a certain route and insist on going that way. She will still try to do so- even if something, or someone, is in her way (an obstruction.) Allow a child this routine.

·   Aspergers children are visual learners and often know something without really understanding. Elizabeth can now visualise spellings but she cannot sound them out and apply strategies- for example, see the word all in ball- it is like each word is separate and there are n't any links between them. Do use multi-sensory teaching of literacy- auditory, kinaesthetic and visual.

Touch

·   Might not like getting their hands dirty.

- May avoid being touched.
- May engage in bouncing and spinning.
- Might rock when stressed (e.g. Elizabeth on the toilet.)
- May not like touching certain materials.

DO:

1. Use wipes- one of Elizabeth's obsessions!
2. Warn the child that you are going to touch them (note that doctors do this so as not to alarm children.)
3. Allow the child to wash themselves under your guidance so you do not touch them with too much point pressure.

Taste

- May only eat certain foods.

DO: Introduce similar foods to ones they like. Introduce small portions. Elizabeth always had to be involved in the full process of food- so we would grow vegetables or she would choose them from a farm; as a result she would eat them. She also cooked/baked lots of foods with me- and as a result ate them!

Smell

- May notice subtle smells and becomes fixated with them. Elizabeth will smell everything if she is unsure.

In conclusion, regarding the senses, many aspergers children notice minute changes, sounds and smells whilst others do not. They often cannot filter out distant sounds/visual distractions and can be/feel 'overloaded' - resulting in them shutting down and focusing on one thing.

MULTI-SENSORY TEACHING

The more senses involved, the more ways information can be transformed and the likelihood of permanent learning. Most people use more than one method but aspergers students do depend upon the visual and may need a different approach when trying to learn and remember something new.

VISUAL

Those with a visual style tend to 'see' words and pictures in their heads. They may prefer to read information to understand it and need to see words on paper when learning spellings.

AUDITORY

Some need to talk about a topic, repeat information aloud or listen to others in order to learn. Elizabeth has to have clear instructions constantly repeated with her name added to ensure she knows what is expected of her.

KINAESTHETIC

Children may need to practise or physically complete an activity to learn successfully. I use physical letters with Elizabeth, she plays with them and forms words.

Practical Ideas For Aspergers Children

To Help With Social Interaction

Speech Therapy- Some Practical Ideas To Help...

This begins with social rules where you have to show the child good behaviour for them to model and then praise them for it- good sitting/looking/listening. A visual timetable can be used to show the child what they are going to do and once it is done take the picture off the timetable and see what is next (they can also put it in a box.)

Focus: turn-taking

You can take turns doing most things- as an activity:

· Find something that interests the child- when Elizabeth was two I used to pass her the jigsaw pieces. By the age of three she was finding it difficult if I wanted/tried to fit a piece so I just 'hovered' around.

· When a child is younger it is a good idea to encourage turn-taking, via toys. Children become attached to toys, sometimes they have a favourite toy- ask them to take turns hugging a toy, the child first and then yourself. This works well with lots of children. However, not with some aspergers children; 'Mousey' could not be prised from Elizabeth, at first, but with time...

· I would take turns stirring cake mixture with Elizabeth, using an egg timer so that she could see how long her turn was. Be firm. Elizabeth was better at taking turns with me but it seemed to be harder with her brother and sharing with others, especially friends, was definitely problematic. It is all about listening, waiting and taking turns- people use gesture and make eye contact and an aspergers child cannot easily pick up on such facial expressions.

Instructions

These must be kept simple; for example I would give Elizabeth an instruction, e.g. "Hug Mousey" then let her tell me what to do- "Brush Mousey." Also I would play snap with cards and encourage Elizabeth to shout "Stop!" when the cards matched. Playing 'Simon Says' is also a good idea as children need to listen carefully to what you are telling them to do, "Touch your toes," but if you don't say, "Simon says.." then they don't do it. Keeping it fun is essential.

Giving Information

Put objects in a bag. Try to identify an object by feeling. Make a few guesses before being told what the object is. Swap roles.

Requests

This starts with simple dressing/undressing- "Vest off," "Knickers, please." Then extend the request, "Can/May I have my vest, please?"

When playing with a ball I would call Elizabeth's name then roll the ball to her. I would ask her to say my name before she rolled it back.

Asking questions and answering

You can begin with asking children simple yes/no questions to gain an answer. Play a hiding game. Hide a toy and ask, "Is it under there?" Look. Try again. Swap roles.

What, Where and Why?

A toy can be used and was, indeed, essential for Elizabeth. "Mousey is happy? Why? How would you feel if that was happening to you? What makes Elizabeth happy/sad?" Extremes like happy and sad do work better, it is the subtle emotions and facial expressions that are more problematic.

Pictures can be used for some areas:

1. Questioning. "What's he doing? Where is it happening?"
"Why is it happening?" is deeper but what is important is that you 'model' responses, via explaining, for a child to learn from so that they can understand why something happens.

2. Emotions and facial expressions. Show a picture of a child- they could be happy/sad. Then have a series of pictures and the child has to pick the appropriate picture to match the situation- for example a child has fallen over so he/she is sad. Use 'Emotions and Facial Expressions' by Helen Rippon - I am now completing it with Elizabeth for the third time. I use facial expression cards all the time with Elizabeth at home.

3. To tell a story- use a sequence of three pictures which tell a story. I use Easylearn's 'Order! Order!' which consists of three pictures on a piece of A4. You draw what happens next in the last box and discuss.

4. To secure the use of prepositions, such as under, on top, in, behind… You can point to the object or use a real toy and place it somewhere in a room. Elizabeth did not have any knowledge of such words as under because if she couldn't clearly see something then it did not exist. I am having this problem with Elizabeth and God, at the moment- "If God is everywhere then why do I have to go to church?"

Improving Auditory Memory and Listening /Attention Skills

A weak area for Elizabeth so I tried:

Making a statement then asking a question to the child, for example, Elizabeth was hungry. She said, "I want a banana, please." What did Elizabeth say?

Recalling objects- Elizabeth could not remember more than one object at a time. When she was three her favourite meal was fish fingers, chips and peas. If it was in front of her then she could recall but if not she was unable to ask for it, fully. So, I would have pictures of each item and then I would take one of the three items away and ask, "What else did Elizabeth eat?"

Expanding to paired work with Alex; read a short story and then give each child an item to hold- when they hear that item mentioned they must hold it up in the air. This worked well with both Elizabeth and Alex together as an older sibling led the way.

Social Stories- this is a short story written in a certain style and format. Each story describes a situation/skill in terms of relevant social cues and common responses. I do invent these depending upon Elizabeth's needs; you can purchase certain books and I have included a list of appropriate resources at the end of part 3. They give people direct information to understand the behaviour of others. These can be used in groups to develop an understanding of emotions and the feelings of others. I am also still completing an emotions workbook with Elizabeth which looks at how to respond to feeling angry or upset.

Comic Strip Conversations- these involve drawing a sequence of cartoon conversations. I use these surrounding an incident which has caused Elizabeth to be upset or angry. Aspergers children (especially those with speech and language needs) cannot explain/understand their own emotions and I always find the heart of the problem lies beneath. By drawing cartoon stick characters and analysing the situation I can ascertain the problem.

Visual Support Timetable For Aspergers Children

This is a clearly defined structure and routine in a physical form- picture and a word. The aim: although life does follow some fixed routine often schools/parents may want variety but this can result in uncertainty and anxiety for those aspergers children. A visual timetable literally breaks down the day and gives advance warning of 'what comes next.'

The child must understand the drawings/what they have to do in this process. This prevents uncooperative behaviour as the child (once they know what to expect) will be able to not fear activities. Imagine being forced to do what everyone else wanted all of the time? As human beings we negotiate- sometimes we may have more power than others or than at other times but we do elude/manage this so we feel as if we have some say. The aspergers child needs help in this area.

Detailed day

A daily timetable can be more detailed. However, once a child can manage you can include less detail. For example:

Morning routine

Picture of toilet/bathroom.
Picture of hands and washing.
Toothbrush.
School clothes.
Specific breakfast on the table

Coat, school bag, scarf/gloves- weather dictated. I do allow my daughter to choose what order to complete the above activities now that she is five years old. However, on weekends I will use different cards with either/or activities.

I also have a little chart which says:
Where is Mummy? Where is Elizabeth?
There are symbols which signify home, work or school. This is used so that Elizabeth knows where I am when she is at school.

Weekly timetable

Elizabeth becomes 'lost' during a school week and wants it to be the weekend. She particularly wants to be at home and finds the school week difficult. So, we use a weekly visual timetable at home.

It shows the important parts of the day in chronological order.

Discuss each activity with the child at the beginning of the day and mention any activities that may change (i.e. because of the weather) to prepare the child for any change.

Once the activity has been finished place it in a box. If an activity was changed then place the replacement alongside/underneath the original picture and place an x over the latter.

When using a timetable at home- add a clock face if needed and a time next to the activity to indicate when it should be completed, in order to stay focused.

I colour code so that Elizabeth can clearly see that she has a lot of time at home and I allow her to construct/draw her own symbols (for example, for ballet) to make it more personal to her- pink and yellow (her favourite colours) act as a visual prompt.

Understanding Different Behaviour In Different Settings

A diagram can be used with your child to consider different types of behaviour in different settings. Elizabeth can see at home that hugs are allowed but when at school (with people you are not close to) then other behaviour is more appropriate. At school, you can wave to people you know but would not hug the Head teacher- shaking hands is an option in this situation.

AT SCHOOL

I can wave to people in my class.

> Don't stand too close to people when talking to them.
>
> Hug/kiss my brother before he goes inside the classroom so he is not embarrassed .
>
> Don't shout when people are near me!

AT HOME

Hugs are allowed.

I can hug my best friends when saying, "Goodbye!"

> I can shake hands with people I know in school.

Friendship

This looks at who you are closest to and I discuss appropriate behaviour with Elizabeth; including personal space and looking at people's faces.

Those I don't like.

_____

Strangers   Postman   Lolli-pop man

Owner of favourite restaurant- 'The Barking Frog.'

Lady who serves me in my local café, 'The Pantry.'

_____

People I Know   My teacher   My friends' parents

Teaching Assistant   Swimming instructor

Ballet teacher

_____

My Class   Those I see in school everyday.

_____

Friends   Girls in my class whom I like.

_____

Family   Mummy   Daddy Alex   Cousins

Nanny and Grandad   Aunties and Uncles

_____

ME   I love myself!

Some Examples of Excellent Organised Support

Parent Support Groups- many local authorities have Autism and Aspergers Parent Groups- these invite all parents/carers to meet similar people, say once a month for two hours for an informative/informal chat and refreshments. Also, there are support group where parents offer support to other parents of 'disabled' children. This is all about befriending and giving people the support which they need.

Sibling Support Groups- an opportunity to meet others in similar situations and have some fun, away from the family situation. There are Learning Disabilities Teams throughout the country which run workshops for siblings of children who have a disability, aged 5-18. There are workshops, then there is time to socialise and outside activities can be arranged and people can keep in touch with their new friends.

Positive Futures- this is a national social inclusion program for children and young people who often miss out on activities; including the opportunity to get involved in sport and other leisure activities. 1:1 support can be provided. It is for those aged 5-24 years.

A.S.D. Link Nurses- Specialist Nurses supporting Children and Families of those who are on the autistic spectrum. Pre-school A.S.D. link nurses meet with you and you can learn about A.S.D. and strategies to aid your child. Then there is a follow-up visit at home. There is some variation in provision between Local Education Authorities as some run similar groups where parents meet/are trained and people meet similar parents. From my experience these nurses are excellent!

Some L.E.A.s have Parent Partnership Services which offer training for schools concerning aspergers (effective communication with parents and disability discrimination.) In my area, for example, there are parent programs for those who have a child with an aspergers diagnosis- 8 weekly sessions covering children 5-7 years and 8-11 years. They can also provide staff training in schools. Many are parents of similar children.

In some parts of the country, they also offer free beauty treatments to parents and carers who have children with Special Educational Needs. This includes facials, pedicures and so on- all aimed at de-stressing. There are also free hypno-psychotherapy sessions available to parents/carers to help with anxiety.

Autism Friendly Screenings at a local cinema. These are aimed at children and young people with autism as well as family/friends and vary countrywide as they are dependent upon local authority funding. The aim is to have a screening every month. Those who have a sensory sensitivity to sound and light can experience the lowering of both in the auditorium. Anyone who needs to move around during the film can as there is a quiet space provided.

Swimming Baths Quiet Night- often available one evening each month. These are designed to give access for children and young people with an aspergers diagnosis, their families and carers. The problem with this is that it is late evening time. My daughter is 4 when I telephone. I point out to the man on the telephone that by the time I get her changed and home bed time would be about 9.15 on a school night. The night runs from 6.30-8.30. My daughter would be in her pyjamas at home by 7, ready for a 12 hour sleep. Still, a good, admirable idea which I will consider when she is older. Only a fraction of the total venue capacity will have access in order to keep noise levels to a minimum. It is aimed at those who cannot generally use swimming baths as they cause 'over stimulation.'

O.S.S.M.E./AUTISM INITIATIVES

This service is excellent and I would highly recommend it. Contact with the service is made by schools or parents and it has to agree funding with the L.E.A. Then there are various steps:

Step 1 Referral- date arranged for the meeting with all parties.
Step 2 Initial Meeting- the sharing of information about the child.
Step 3 Observation and strategy meeting- the service observe the child and offer advice to staff; report written/recommendations are made.
Step 4- Final conference- report discussed and action planned.
Step 5- Evaluation- monitored on a termly basis.

Disability Living Allowance

This is a benefit for people with an illness or disability- in Elizabeth's case help getting around or/and help with personal care. It is available to all, regardless of family income/savings and can help to pay for any extra help your child may need; for example, small group swimming lessons.

I had to detail the help she needs most of the time. She has good/bad days. It can be upsetting to fill in- personal questions and seeing it all documented in black and white, can hit a parent hard! They do provide help to fill in the claim form and you can speak to someone concerning general advice. You can be pointed in the right direction with regards to organisations that can be of further assistance.

Elizabeth needs someone with her to ensure that she is safe/can find her way around in unfamiliar places. With regards to personal care- she needs more help/supervision than other children of the same age who do not have her particular needs. Such help can be washing, dressing, using the toilet, (don't I know it!) communicating with other people; it can include reminding, prompting, encouraging to do things during the day and night. It can include attention with bodily functions several times at short intervals right through the day/more than once a night or once for a prolonged period.

In conclusion, what is important is that all family members create a positive environment for the aspergers child- all working together with consistency. I could not do what I do without my husband and son as they approach Elizabeth in rather a different way than I - with their different personalities; between us we are succeeding with her and have a reasonably adjusted child. So, let us end on a positive note…

Strengths of Aspergers Children

Aspergers children do have a 'different' look or 'take' on the world. If you think about all being the same and how boring life would be, then that helps. Some could be visionaries- people who have made a difference to the world by seeing things differently.

They have an honesty which is quite refreshing in today's world and make loyal friends forever!

They may have a talent for learning facts and skills. Elizabeth pays attention to fine detail and is very artistic.

Employers may like their focus on detail/chosen activity- way after others give up, they still have the determination to succeed and be independent.

Now, that all sounds good, does n't it?

Useful Resources

Baldwin, L. (2008) Receptive Language Difficulties. Practical Strategies to Help Children Understand Spoken Language. LDA: Cambridge.

Browning Wroe, Jo and Holliday, Carol. (2009 reprint) Forest of Feelings. Understanding and Exploring Emotions. LDA: Nottingham.

Cohen, D. and Jaderberg, L. (2008) Social Skills For Primary Pupils 1. Seven one-hour sessions to help pupils develop social awareness and personal responsibility. LDA: Nottingham.

Cohen, D. and Jaderberg, L. (2008) Social Skills For Primary Pupils 2. Seven one-hour sessions to help pupils develop social awareness and personal responsibility. LDA: Nottingham.

Easylearn. Order!Order! Teach Child Essential Sequencing Skills. Easylearn: Nottinghamshire.

Fleetham, Mike. (2009 reprint) Thinking Stories to Wake Up Your Mind. LDA: Nottingham.

Rippon, Helen. (undated) Pragmatics/Semantics 1. Emotions and Facial Expressions. Black Sheep Press: W.Yorks.

Schroeder, Alison. (2009 reprint) Time To Talk. A Programme to Develop Oral and Social Interaction Skills at Reception and Key Stage One. LDA: Nottingham.

Sheratt, David. (2009 reprint) How to…Support and Teach Children on the Autism Spectrum. LDA: Nottingham.

The National Autistic Society. 0845 070 4004 autismhelpline@nas.org.uk

About the Author

Colette McCoy has been a teacher for 17 years. She has worked for various education authorities as a special needs teacher- teaching and supporting children; providing advice/ workshops for parents; training both teachers and teaching assistants from schools/colleges. She lives in Ainsdale, Southport, with her husband, Terry, and has two young children- Alexander and Elizabeth.

CPSIA information can be obtained at www.ICGtesting.com
Printed in the USA
LVOW03s1039061114

412271LV00015B/1/P